Alpha

Alpha

A Case Study in Upgrading

Leonard P.R. Granick
Lee E. Jacobson
Robert Bruce Greaux
New Careers Systems Institute, Inc.

Lexington Books
D.C. Heath and Company
Lexington, Massachusetts
Toronto London

Library of Congress Cataloging in Publication Data

Granick, Leonard P.R.
  Alpha: a case study in upgrading.

  Includes bibliographical references.
  1. Employees, Training of—Case studies. 2. Promotions—Case studies. 3. Manpower policy—Case studies. I. Jacobson, Lee E., joint author. II. Greaux, Robert Bruce, joint author. III. Title.
  HF5549.5.T7G56   1975   658.31'4   74-297
  ISBN 0-669-91843-1

Copyright © 1973 by New Careers Systems Institute, Inc.
Copyright © 1975 by D.C. Heath and Company.

Reproduction in whole or in part permitted for any purpose of the United States Government.

All rights reserved. No part of this publication may be reproduced or transmitted in any form or by any means, electronic or mechanical, including photocopy, recording, or any information storage or retrieval system, without permission in writing from the publisher. The provision of the United States Government constitutes the only exception to this prohibition. This report on a special manpower project was prepared under a contract with the Manpower Administration, U.S. Department of Labor, under the authority of the Manpower Development and Training Act. Organizations undertaking such projects under Government sponsorship are encouraged to express their own judgment freely. Therefore, points of view or opinions stated in this document do not necessarily represent the official position or policy of the Department of Labor.

Published simultaneously in Canada

Printed in the United States of America

International Standard Book Number: 0-669-91843-1

Library of Congress Catalog Card Number: 74-297

RIDER COLLEGE LIBRARY

TABLE OF CONTENTS

		Page
	Foreword by *Frank Riessman*	1
I	UPGRADING ISSUES AND MANPOWER POLICY	5

This chapter discusses general manpower issues related to upgrading and possible impacts that might be anticipated from carrying out a given policy. The company itself provides a data input which characterizes the possible consequences of a specific manpower program mix.

II	ALPHA PLASTICS PRINTING CO., INC.	13

A brief history of a small-sized, low-wage paying firm experiencing difficulty in securing high skilled employees is provided. As an "employer of last resort," the company had been unsuccessful in joining the interests of the disadvantaged, recruited from the local Black community, with its own desire to maximize its profitability.

III	UPGRADE VARIABLES AND CONDITIONS	29

In this chapter the company is described typologically as it relates to a developing knowledge regarding the variables and conditions that affect the development of upgrade models in industry.

IV	JOB REDESIGN AND JOB LADDER DEVELOPMENT	51

To permit employee upgrading, a redesign of each job and the job ladder was undertaken. Of necessity, the redesign had to be restricted by the specifics of the company's productive procedures.

Redesigning the Jobs

Certifying the Jobs

Developing Job Ladders

Wage Scales

V	PROGRAM PARAMETERS	63

Employees were hired by the company (as before) entering the program on a "first come, first serve" basis. A variety of program choices were available to both new and present employees, including GED or skills training (with or without GED), leading to printer or lamination operator positions.

Recruitment and Hiring

Program Choices

Release Time

Skill Training and Related Instruction

Trainer Training

		Page
V	PROGRAM PARAMETERS (Cont'd)	
	Basic Education	
	Progression Steps	
	Supportive Services	
	Employer Commitment	
VI	PROGRAM PARTICIPANTS	75

New employees entering the upgrade program (employee-trainees) are described in detail and contrasted with all other new hires (non-program) and applicants (not hired) during the same period. Senior employees who took part in the program are also described. New employees include (1) older Black workers who had not been able to find and/or hold onto higher paying jobs, (2) younger Black workers in the labor force for a short period of time and (3) veterans and workers entering the labor force for the first time.

VII	SHORT-TERM QUANTITATIVE RESULTS AND FINDINGS	95

The findings of a short term, three-month follow-up are reported. The results are favorable in that printers were trained and subsequently promoted. Other trainees, at all stages of skills development, also were trained and thereafter earned considerably higher wages. For employees separating from the company before completing training, long periods of unemployment occurred, and subsequent jobs were not related in skills to the training received.

VIII	ECONOMIC EFFECTS OF UPGRADING FOR COMPANY	119

This chapter deals with economic benefits which can result from upgrading. In this demonstration at Alpha, some direct production gains were observed, as well as benefits from reduced turnover.

IX	LONG-TERM FOLLOW-UP	133

This chapter describes a one year follow-up. In general, the upgraded employees at Alpha held onto their jobs and received further wage gains. A reorganization displaced some of the program employees who found higher paying jobs elsewhere but not in the same line of work. The attitudes of the company had not changed. In fact, the success of the program reinforced some negative behaviors toward the untrained men in entry level employment.

		Page
X	POLICY FINDINGS, UPGRADE CONDITIONS AND VARIABLES	141

    Absence of Displacement Concerns
    Resolution of Employer-Employee Needs
        Employer Rationale
        Employer Assessment
        Employee Participation
        Wage Differentials
        Paid Release Time
        Commensurate Wage Increases
        Long Term Effects of Program
        Employee Experiences
        Employee Discipline
        Foremen and Supervisors
    Institutional Changes
        Entry Level Requirements/Attitudes
        Educational Credentials
    Non-Continuance of Upgrade Project
        Costs
    Industry Focused Technology

APPENDIX A	R & D TYPOLOGY OF INDUSTRIAL UPGRADING CONDITIONS AND VARIABLES	161
APPENDIX B	SUPPORTIVE SERVICES	173
APPENDIX C	GENERAL EDUCATION DEVELOPMENT (GED) PROGRAM	185
APPENDIX D	JOB TASK ANALYSIS	205

Alpha

Foreword

The workers appearing at Alpha's front gate were no different than tens of thousands who seek work—or are frozen into dead-end jobs—every year in American factories. The authors of this volume provide a well-documented, analytic view of the existent barriers and likely outcomes of current efforts to upgrade these workers.

Granick, Jacobson, and Greaux argue persuasively that when something more in the way of training and *opportunity* is offered, the ordinary hard-core worker can be employed in a high-skill job, performing as well or better than the employer expects. They demonstrate that where such "industry-focused" techniques as job redesign and reasonable job progression ladders are set into place we can anticipate rapid returns.

Surprisingly, the United States is one of the few major countries in which it is not government policy to continuously seek out methods for the improvement of our workforce. Despite a recent HEW-sponsored monograph detailing the deterioration of the quality of work life and worker outlook, no dramatic change in policy has been forthcoming.

In recent years, at least three new and different efforts of interest have been initiated: the New Careers approach, typified by Alpha; the HIT (High Intensity Training) approach; and the TIPP (Training Incentive Payments Plan) approach. HIT is a one-job-step, forty-hour upgrade training model, with job redesign features. TIPP is fundamentally an employer reimbursement strategy to offset the costs to the employer of successful upgrading. Each of these approaches carries lessons for the other. The TIPP approach says to the employer, "O.K., if you see a need and a benefit to you from upgrading your workforce, go ahead and do it. We will reimburse you at x percent, everytime you're successful" (as measured by the wage gain for the upgraded employee). Some employers go right ahead and do it, while many others don't or can't do it.

For those who can't by themselves, HIT is a possibility. From 1966 to 1970, some 3,500 employees in a variety of industries were involved in HIT programs. Most were upgraded one step, with a wage gain after forty hours of training and support. While successful as far as it went, HIT had its limitations. Once employees were promoted there was no *multiplier effect.* Neither program participants nor nonparticipants advanced much beyond the initial job jump.

The Alpha approach was more intensive than HIT; it involved both job redesign and job restructuring. Classroom and OJT were provided, as were education, counseling, and supportive services. Each job step was linked and there were progressive increments throughout.

The returns were dramatic; the participants climbed the ladder to the top. The program "over-succeeded" in that it produced too many "successful" candidates. The employer was overwhelmed.

What is important here is the potential power of upgrading technology. Whereas it ordinarily takes four years and then some to qualify a high-skilled employee at Alpha (a plastics printer), the objective was achieved in six to nine months.

Industry is not the *only* potential benefactor of these concepts; the human services sector may benefit as well. In New York City, for example, 400 nurses aides in the municipal hospitals began a fourteen-month, part-time training course in licensed practical nursing. They spent half of the course time at work, and the other half in classroom or clinical instruction. Ninety-one percent successfully completed the course. The associated research indicates that their performance was equal to, or better, than LPNs trained in a traditional model.

Foreword

Here, as in previous studies, lack of education credentials is found to be irrelevant to upgrading, although it may be a formal barrier to credentialization. In the LPN program, although a considerable number of aides had reading handicaps, there was little evidence that the handicaps served as a barrier to their eventual success.

In neither Alpha, HIT, nor TIPP is education a noticeable constraint to upgrading. In the factory, work is organized and commanded by the productive machinery of the plant. A high school education or reading skills, while necessary for some jobs, are not prerequisites for most high-skill jobs in a factory. The rules and standards are communicated by verbal instruction and example—e.g., learning when to turn a lever, inspect quality, run a test, lead a crew, observe safety rules. In fact, many of the employees in these studies are dropouts. Schools have failed to service them, and they are unlikely to return. Nonetheless, they are learning all the time.

Alpha provides many lessons for us. The book should be read, studied, and debated as to its conclusions.

Frank Riessman
Queens College

1
Upgrading Issues and Manpower Policy

The increasing emphasis on upgrading in federal manpower programs is closely related to the deployment of more wide-ranging techniques and support for aiding disadvantaged members of the labor force and of assuring equal employment opportunities for all races. In part, upgrading is the response of the Manpower Administration to fulfilling this need by developing programs to assist the several million workers who are employed full time but remain below the poverty income level. The position of some analysts holds that training for advancement to higher-pay jobs enables many of these "working poor" to move up to higher incomes. As such, upgrading is in response to the dissatisfactions expressed by disadvantaged workers who have found themselves receiving government subsidy for training in low-level, "dead-end" jobs.[1] Some economists believe that upgrade programs can be used to remove skill shortages by improving the matching

---

[1] William Kolberg, "Upgrading the Working Poor," MANPOWER, November, 1969.
Ray Marshall, "Reflections on Upgrading," MANPOWER, January, 1970.

of skills in the supply and demand of the labor market.[2] Nonetheless, there is concern that non-subsidized, low-income workers may be displaced from their accustomed jobs by the subsidization of the disadvantaged, resulting in a sum zero gain. These concerns may be discounted in companies where there are shortages of higher skills. Displacement risks tend not to occur, for the reason that there is sufficient job promotion space for both groups. In industries without skill shortages and minimal promotion space, the displacement concern remains a relevant issue. What emerges, as related to displacement, is who will get available jobs.

Theoretically, then, there are displacement risks. Federal subsidies may act to lower the relative price of labor for one group of employees, thereby decreasing its capital-labor ratio to the company. Presumably, this could result in preferential recruitment and hiring of disadvantaged workers. Unless there is also an increase in total employment for the company, there may be pressures toward displacement of non-subsidized workers, especially in non-union shops.[3]

Upgrading has also been utilized as a strategy to increase the representation of racial minorities in skilled jobs. Industry has not purposefully sought to develop and upgrade lower-level employees. Industry has been reluctant to conduct special training or develop methods to put in place upward mobility systems.

If the non-subsidized employee is allowed to move up, it is possible for his position to be filled by one of those considered disadvantaged. However, if the higher skilled jobs are taken by present non-subsidized employees, then only the lower skilled jobs are left. Under this condition, "equal opportunity" is difficult to achieve for large numbers of the disadvantaged. If the disadvantaged are subsidized, thereby largely excluding the "working poor" from participation in upgrade programs, the present non-subsidized employees may feel that they have been subject to discrimination. Several questions remain: Will both groups of workers take advantage of an upward mobility system or will the new hire, the previously unemployed disadvantaged, find

---

2 Lester Thurow, "The Role of Manpower Policy in Achieving Aggregate Goals," in Robert Gordon (Ed.), TOWARD A MANPOWER POLICY, New York: Wiley, 1967.

3 Daniel S. Hamermesh, ECONOMIC ASPECTS OF MANPOWER TRAINING PROGRAMS: THEORY AND POLICY, Lexington, Mass: Heath, 1971.

that they have merely taken over the "dead-end" job slot of the promoted employees? Does such a worker have to wait for the senior employee to quit, for his retirement, death, dismemberment, or for a surge of new jobs before he can be promoted as well?

These questions may be roughly stated as three alternative strategies in upgrade programming:

1. *Upgrading as it relates to training unemployed workers for entry level jobs:* One assumption is that these new employees could then move up as part of the normal progression procedure within the company. Their mobility, of course, would vary in accordance with specific mobility factors of the industry, such as the employee's rank order in the upgrade queue.

Resistance to pursuing this strategy comes from data which indicate that these jobs are "dead-end."

2. *Upgrading as it relates to training entry level employees for higher skilled jobs:* These upgraded workers would occupy the higher skill jobs, vacating their present jobs for unemployed workers. This assumes that there are a sufficient number of higher skilled jobs and that the upgrading of entry level employees can occur rapidly, not causing excessive delays before the unemployed are brought into the labor force. Others argue that whether the entry level positions are occupied by subsidized or non-subsidized employees, present upgrade routes are replete with numerous outdated barriers. They argue that upgrade routes require something more than traditional OJT or long-term apprenticeship training, perhaps some such *industry-focused* technique as job redesign, job progression ladders, even including the revision of outdated credential requirements.[4]

3. *Upgrading as it relates to training unemployed workers directly for higher skilled jobs:* The difficulties attendant upon adopting this strategy are multifold. Problems include the resistance of employers and unions to skipping over their present work force (senior employees) in favor of the disadvantaged, and the potential political and

---

4 Frank Riessman and Hermine Popper, UP FROM POVERTY, New York: Harper & Row, 1968.

Arthur W. Kirsch and Donald D. Cooke, UPGRADING THE WORKFORCE: PROBLEMS AND POSSIBILITIES, New York: E. F. Shelly, 1971.

National Manpower Policy Task Force, CONFERENCE ON UPGRADING AND NEW CAREERS, Department of Labor, 1970.

social response against "favoritism" on the part of the employed versus the disadvantaged. As well, there is the assumed relatively higher cost of pursuing this approach as against the cost of upgrading the present work force. This third alternative does not answer the spokesmen for the disadvantaged. Their contention is that equal opportunity cannot occur unless there is *equal* (concurrent) access to higher skilled jobs and that other approaches, used to date, build-in and enhance pre-existent inequities in upgrading opportunities.

*

What combination of these three strategies should be pursued, and under what conditions should that combination be varied?

Of particular interest in this report is the potential effect of these manpower strategies as they may impact on specific firms. In this context, Alpha Plastics Printing Co., Inc. provides an opportunity to study the more specific effects of some of these alternatives.

This report on Alpha is based on the case study method. As such, it generates specific information (and related questions) about some of the variables to be identified and studied before more generic upgrading models can be developed, installed and tested in a wider range of private industrial settings. *This report on Alpha is limited as to addressing broad policy questions, because it deals in detail only with the special needs and problems of one upgrading model in one plant. The Alpha experience does not allow for broad generalizations about upgrading systems in a wider range of industries.*

In the Alpha study, an *industry-focused* upgrading model based on job redesign was installed and studied. The program provided for rapid promotion to higher skill jobs and wage increases for senior employees and new hires, concurrently.

There were several assumptions underlying the upgrade program at Alpha:

1. In order to accelerate the promotion of new and senior employees, it was assumed that it would be necessary to *modernize* or *supersede* the traditional apprenticeship upgrading mode. This assumption argued that it was necessary to minimize the intrinsic requirements of lengthy training for program success.

To facilitate promotion, industry-focused upgrade development techniques were employed and supported by a mixed training model of vestibule and specialized OJT.

2. The specific form of industry-focused techniques employed would be determined by the specific industry and occupations within the plant. At Alpha, the choice was markedly affected by the company's organization of production. Alpha's method of producing goods was based on a crew-machine form of productive organization. The size of the large presses and laminator-embossers and the machine process itself determined: (a) the type of work performed by each of the men in the crew, and (b) the physical placement and location of work stations separating one man from the other.

The setting was, therefore, judged inappropriate for such industry-focused techniques as job enrichment, whole work units, or job expansion techniques. Similarly, the method of operation and tending of the equipment did not lend itself to job fractionalization. The machine did much of the work; the men already had spurts of "idle time." The wage costs prohibited assignment of another man to the crew, limiting crew-size expansion.

The *skills gap* between entry level and printer or operator was "bridged" by a job progression ladder based on a job redesign upgrade model. This permitted the lower skilled crew members to learn the higher skilled job functions (printer or operator) as part of their regular work routines (backed by training).

3. It was assumed that some *employee-focused* techniques (counseling, basic education and supportive services) would be required. The scope of these techniques was nonetheless constrained -- to mainly providing employee assistance in offering supports that would help them in moving up the progression ladder. As such, the supports were job-centered and work related. The decision to constrain supportive services in this manner was based on such factors as:

a. The assumption that only a few employees would voluntarily ask for personal counseling. This expectancy was based upon the previous experience of the contractor in private industry and the public sector programming. It was consistent with Alpha's own experience.

b. The observation that the acquisition of higher level skills (of printers and operators) was not based primarily on having proficient educational skills in mathematics or science, or an extensive need to comprehend written materials. It would only be necessary to be able to read and understand the manuals. Consequently, the basic education focus was held to reading comprehension and sixth grade mathematics.

c. The expectancy that entry level employees, because of prolonged periods of unemployment, would need supportive services in the form of financial and legal assistance. In addition, supportive services were considered necessary in providing back-up supports for already successful employees. If extended to entry level employee-trainees, these services could possibly reduce turnover and "protect" the training investment.

*

It was assumed that should the model effectively accelerate the progression process *concurrently* for both senior employees and new hires, it would, on a per person cost, be an incentive for the employer to adopt the program on a continuing basis. As such, the cost picture would be favorable in contrast to the traditional method of first upgrading present employees, then training new hires for entry level jobs and, subsequently, providing additional training for promotion from entry level positions.

Having designed and installed the upgrade model, it would then be possible to observe, measure and address questions regarding those issues which are relevant to policy planning.

1. Since the development of the upgrade program was subsidized by the contractor (in terms of technical expertness and employer protection), would the program be adopted and become employer supported when the contractor completed its work and withdrew?

As an incentive to continuance, the contractor would attempt to demonstrate the effectiveness of the program and would train the company's personnel in the operation of the program. The instrumentalities which were developed -- training plans, manuals, and curricula -- could be used by these trained personnel for upgrading.

2. Is it possible to bridge the interests of the employer with those of the employee by a commitment to upgrade the employee in return for improvements in production and, consequently, in profits?

Interest was focused on the relationship between the problems and needs of the employer and those of the worker, especially the entry level, least skilled minority employee.

It was apparent that Alpha had been experiencing difficulty in bringing together these two "need areas," as evidenced by high turnover, complaints about skill shortages, and fall-offs in quality and efficiency of production.

3. Which employees would choose to participate? What would be the response to concurrent upgrading of new and senior employees on the part of the union, management, and co-workers?

Would present employees completely subsume all the upgrade positions, leaving none for the newly hired? Who would come in to replace the upgraded employee?

4. Do these upgrade efforts have any long-term effects? What about one year later? Are the upgraded employees integral to the company's internal labor force or have they moved on to other jobs? What happens to those who leave? Are they upwardly mobile? What would be their subsequent employment experience in terms of the jobs they held and the monies they earned?

In short, does the interim adjustment of existing manpower practices within a company during the demonstration phase produce subsequent, more stable *institutional* adjustment of the company's policies and practices? Does the company sustain the changes in production processes, allocation of company fiscal resources, employee benefits, personnel practices, or qualifications for entry level hiring?

Summary

Single company case study methods in research related to federal manpower policies are intrinsically limited with respect to their ability to generalize much beyond the immediate company experience. However, they do provide some valuable insight as to the conditions and variables that impact upon manpower policies. As to methods of upgrading, industry-focused upgrade technologies may be developed and improved upon.

The single company study also helps to identify factors affecting the long-term durability of subsidized programs, as to: (a) whether specific upgrade programming policies equally benefit the disadvantaged and senior (present) work force, and (b) whether upgrading can generate economic benefits to the company. The secondary effects of these policies on the company are viewed institutionally in terms of personnel practices, qualifications, and the allocation of its own fiscal resources.

2
Alpha Plastics Printing Co., Inc.

Introduction

New Brunswick's commercial center is on George and French Streets. Off French, running a mile or more to Route 1, is the "Jersey Strip." Some forty-two factories, including Alpha Plastics Printing Co., Inc.,[1] line this artery. Along Route 1 are the spacious offices and industrial plants of some of America's largest corporations: Johnson and Johnson, Squibb, and Ford Motor Company. Along the Jersey Strip are the lesser-known, by-and-large lower wage-paying employers.

An estimated 11,000 persons are employed in New Brunswick, a great many of whom reside in neighboring communities. In the community, poverty is concentrated in New Brunswick and Perth Amboy.

---

1 In the interest of anonymity, Alpha Plastic Printing Co., Inc. is a pseudonym for the R & D site. The nature of the product and other factors are accurately reported.

These municipalities contain over one-half of the county's poor, including Blacks, recent Puerto Rican immigrants and a large ethnic mixture of Polish, Italian, Hungarian, Russian and Irish. In 1959, 28.5% of the non-white families in New Brunswick earned under $3,000, compared to 3.3% of the white population.[2]

In education, the rate for adults with less than eight years of schooling was 37% for Blacks and 27% for whites. The large number of foreign born whites in the city was probably one of the contributing factors to the high percentage of whites.[3]

Unemployment rates in the city for 1959 are of interest (see Table 2.1). Of a total of 11,091 civilians (male) in the labor force, 1,006 were unemployed in 1959, an overall rate of 9.1%. In the three census tracts demarcating the Black ghetto in New Brunswick, the rate was 14%. Relative to other ethnic minorities, the unemployment data for Blacks indicate an overall figure small in numerical size but relatively high in rate.

New Brunswick Blacks are a main source of labor as operatives and kindred workers (general factory helpers), as private household workers, or as laborers. They occupy many of the entry level jobs within the two main industrial complexes centered in New Brunswick on the Jersey Strip and just outside the city on Route 1.

Other studies have related these occupations to low income and unsteady employment. However, the wage level and the degree of job security (e.g., as operatives) vary greatly according to industry, type of union organization, and by size of firm.

At the time of the demonstration, in Alpha Plastics Printing Company, Inc. (Alpha), most of the low-level positions were occupied by Blacks who lived less than a mile from the plant.[4] Established 13

---

[2] Georgiana M. Smith, AN OUTLINE OF POVERTY IN MIDDLESEX COUNTY, N. J., Middlesex County Economic Opportunity Corporation, 1967, pp. 12, 17.

[3] Smith, op. cit., p. 42.

[4] The French Street area has a concentration of foreign born residents, more than half of whom, as of the 1960 U. S. census, were Hungarians. White residents, on the whole, are considerably older than non-whites, with smaller sized households and somewhat higher family incomes. They are longer term residents of the city. Their children have grown up and settled outside of New Brunswick. The Hungarian revolt resulted in an influx of younger emigres who relocated in the area. Notwithstanding these differential population characteristics of the city, the primary labor force at Alpha is Black.

years ago, the New Brunswick plant in 1970 employed better than 150 blue-collar workers on three shifts 5½ days a week.

Most of the managerial staff and key production personnel (printers) resided thirty miles away in the Trenton, New Jersey area, the site of the original plant, where Alpha began printing plastics at its founding in 1941. The Trenton plant, cut back three years ago, only produced adhesive-backed vinyls, about 20% of Alpha's product line, as of the time of this study.

Managerial Organization

The company was founded in Trenton by the current President's father. Though a stock corporation, it has remained a family-held business. Of the several family members at work in 1967, only the President was currently active at the time of the demonstration.

During the time covered by this study, the General Manager was in charge of all engineering design changes to the equipment. He was also directly involved in product development. As such, he ran the total operation, reporting only to the President of the company. The supervisor reported directly to the General Manager and served as his assistant; he maintained all production schedules, and directly participated in press setup to maintain quality control on special orders.

The Alpha manufacturing units were organized into a hierarchy which resembled the organizational diagram shown in Figure 2.1. In the production unit, there was a supervisor on the first shift (and assistant supervisors on other shifts) to whom all foremen reported. The lamination operator and the printer were in charge of three-man crews, except for one six-color press which required a four-man crew.

Plastic Print Business

Alpha was known as a converter in the plastics industry. The company produced printed plastic "goods" which were later turned into finished products by manufacturers of umbrellas, tablecloths, upholstery, and wearing apparel. Alpha furnished plastic roll-form goods to these manufacturers in 1200 different patterns, in a number of finishes (whether embossed or laminated), in as many as six colors. Ninety percent of its product was supplied to some 70 finishers in the form of large rolls of printed plastics. Vinyls and nylon accounted for about 40% of its product; polyethylene (poly) for about 60%.

Alpha extruded its own film from plastic pellets (about the size of peas) to the extent of seven million pounds of extruded film each year. The extruded film in three widths (54, 72, and 87 inches) was then laminated and embossed (i.e., surfaced and lined). As a rule, the last step in the process was printing. Alpha had six presses (four in New Brunswick, two in Trenton). One press could print the roll-fed plastic film in as many as six colors by the rotogravure method; the rest were two- or four-color presses.

According to the company, over the years, Alpha had tended toward a specialization in poly goods.[5] This specialization had helped the company maintain poly at virtually the same price of $.60 a pound for more than ten years. The consequence for other converters unable to specialize had been bankruptcy or conversion to the production of other plastic goods. The need to maintain the price of poly was the result of pressure from the market place. Most of the finished products made of this material were sold in chain stores at no more than $1 retail. Such chain operations as five-and-dime stores permitted a given amount of counter space to the $1 item or they removed it from sale.

Alpha had maintained its pricing structure in the face of a 100% rise in the cost of labor by upgrading the technology employed in its New Brunswick operation. These changes in technology over a ten-year period could be seen in the production increases in printing; poly had risen from 55 to 95, and vinyl from 30 to 35 yards-per-minute.

This ten-year change did not appreciably affect the *percentage differentials*[6] which made up the cost of goods sold.

---

5 Film is considered as goods once it has been laminated-embossed and printed.

6 Of recent years, "actual" profit had been about 2% because of cash flow needs imposed by the bank. That is, goods were sold below fair rates to maintain given amounts in the account. This difference can be seen as an overhead charge.

Alpha Plastics Printing Co., Inc.

Item	% of Sale Price
Raw Materials	55
Overhead	23
Labor	12
Profit	10

The first three figures had remained virtually unchanged, little affected by the type and quality of the goods produced. The amount of goods produced did affect the labor costs per pound, the amount of profit being affected by the amount of production as well as its quality. Actual labor costs (cost-per-pound of goods produced) had remained relatively fixed because increases in the cost of labor had been offset by increases in production. These increases had not affected the quality of first-line goods produced until 1968. The quality of such goods had increased through the years to a high of 95% in 1968 and dropped off thereafter. Goods were costed by grade, as follows:

Type	Cost to Finisher
First quality	100
Standard	85
Promotion	70
Second	Variable

Briefly explained, this meant that goods costing the finisher $.60/lb., if standard in grade, were billed at 15% less, or $.51/lb. Since 95% of all goods produced were first quality (on which the profit margin of 10% was predicated), the sale of standard quality represented a net loss of $.03/lb. These figures indicate that goods produced below first quality seriously affected overall profitability.

The ability of the print crew to produce first quality goods at high rates of production (e.g., at an average of 60 yards-per-minute) was crucial to Alpha's profit structure. As might be expected, Alpha organized its work force on the floor to support its print crews; all other processes served this operation (see Figure 2.2).

When two- or four-color goods were produced, three men operated the press. When six colors were run, the crew size was increased to include an assistant (B printer). A similar crew-type operation was employed in lamination-embossing and in extrusion. The importance vested in the print department (supported by the need for greater skills) was partly reflected in the higher salaries for printers (see Table 2.2).

Symptoms Of Trouble

Despite Alpha's engineering capability in improving the productivity of its old presses, it became clear early in 1969 that production could not be sustained at this elevated rate. The source of the difficulty was two-fold: a shortage of skilled printers and poor quality of work as a result of high turnover in entry level positions. In mid-1968, Alpha lost 6 printers (40% of its printers) who left together with one of the foremen to join another company. Alpha was faced with the problems of finding substitute printers and made some minor but insufficient manpower adjustments by bringing men in from its Trenton plant and by hiring others where they could. The shortage of these higher skilled employees remained and its consequence was reflected in lower production. (Difficulties in retaining entry level employees are discussed later in this chapter.)

Coincidentally, there was an increase in the failure to achieve first quality goods. Increasing amounts of poor quality yardage were being run without being flagged and stopped. This problem had surfaced earlier than 1969 and the organization of the crew was shifted so that the more experienced man could work at the physically easier job of cutter rather than backtender. The position of the cutter allowed him to inspect the goods coming off the opposite side of the press (which could not be seen by the printer). This could only be done if the cutter remained on the job. High turnover affected the ability of such a man to perform the quality control function.

Quality production falloffs resulted from the need to have the more experienced man cover the new man's position. The printer had to move off his station to help both of his crew members do their jobs.

The "New" Work Force

In a retrospective study of turnover rates for 1969, the contractor found that of 289 new hires 28% of the "new" work force left within three weeks, 59% in the first month, only 14% remaining after six months. It was continuously necessary to recruit new hires to fill vacated production job positions (see Table 2.3).

The changing composition of Alpha's labor force, management agreed, especially at entry level, was a major problem. When it had moved most of its operation from Trenton, Alpha had brought many of its key production workers to New Brunswick. The rest it had recruited locally. These low-skilled job vacancies were filled through newspaper ads, and, on occasion, the local office of the State Employment Service (SES) and the local poverty agency. Most of its hires, however, were walk-ins, who were referred by friends in the Black community, or saw the "men wanted" sign posted at the front of the building.

The starting wage in the outlying area of the city was $2.50 an hour (minimum). At that time, Alpha paid between $1.90 and $2.10 an hour. One State Employment Service (SES) officer who knew the firm indicated Alpha was considered an "employer of last resort." Workers came to Alpha, as the SES officer had surmised, only after they had asked about jobs at more than one plant along the Jersey Strip and Route 1.

It was not possible to compare the work force at Alpha directly with other small manufacturers in the immediate area, many of whom paid similar low wages. Since the men moved back and forth between these employers, Alpha employees were probably similar to those of other small manufacturers who require virtually unskilled male help to produce their product.

Higher wages were paid by the larger corporations in the outlying areas, especially those located along Route 1. These companies were reputed to be selective in their hiring and they usually had few job openings. The men who finally came to Alpha reported that they had been told by these companies that there were no job openings.

Low wage-paying factory jobs, such as those offered by Alpha, usually drew the younger inexperienced worker, as well as those older men who had not been able to find and hold on to a higher paying job. This latter group was generally composed of men with families who had been employed in a number of low skill jobs as helpers, material handlers, and warehouse workers.

Many of Alpha's workers were new to the work force, having recently been released from the armed services. Others had held a succession of casual jobs (e.g., checker in a supermarket, delivery man, etc.). For others, it was their sixth or seventh job in two or three years. Many had been unemployed for three months or longer. Almost all of them came from the New Brunswick area. A few were recruited from the Trenton area, moving between work and home in car pools.

No accurate analysis of the characteristics of this work group could be undertaken prior to the initiation of the Alpha project. The employment applications filled in by many workers were incomplete. None of them had been verified. If those employed before 1970 were similar to those recruited for the project,[7] it is likely that more than half were high school dropouts. A few had experienced some brush with the law. Some had been charged with major crimes, but only a few had spent time in jail. At least one man was on parole.

Men showing up on Alpha's doorstep, those without experience in the plastics industry, were Black or Puerto Rican. Since many of the latter group do not speak English, mostly Blacks (about 85%) were hired into entry factory jobs involving the direct production of goods. Some Puerto Ricans were hired to work in the warehouse, but none were hired to work in printing or laminating-embossing. Because of the proximity of Rutgers University, the balance of the labor force consisted of some younger whites hired part-time to work during the summer months. Other whites (non-students) were generally assigned to such units as strikeoff (a unit which checked new patterns) for which "greater skills were required." Alpha frequently filled its manpower requisitions with little or no checking of qualifications. If a man appeared to be in good health and was not color

---

[7] Workers for the project were recruited on a "first come, first serve" basis. However, it cannot be fully assumed that no significant difference existed between those recruited prior to 1970 and those recruited for employment thereafter. For example, there was a marked increase in Puerto Rican applicants in late 1970, an overflow from increasingly higher unemployment rates in the Perth Amboy area.

blind, he was put to work for relatively small wages (see Table 2.2).

For the men "who made it" (the old timers from Trenton), the company was willing to extend itself. The older worker went to the General Manager if he had a problem, personal or otherwise. He was known to "twist a banker's arm" to get loans for employees seeking to buy homes. More than once, he had gotten an older employee the help he needed (generally, domestic; sometimes, alcoholism) from a social service agency. On the other hand, the President of the company was known to have reprimanded employees for "loitering" or for sloppy housekeeping. On several occasions, he was reported to have run a quality control check on the production standards of given workers.

In 30 days, all workers were required to join the local union. Management indicated that, except for pay, very few contract disputes disrupted their relationship with the union. In reviewing grievances for 1969, it was clear that most disputes were settled off the record. In effect, the older, senior worker received protection while the newer worker was frequently dismissed for relatively unsubstantiated causes. Few of the discharged newer workers had ever filed a grievance with the union. The union, generally, did not deny them this right. Frequently, workers were not aware of their grievance rights, or were unwilling to pursue the matter.

It was the management's view that production and quality control problems were the result of employee motivation and insufficient education and skills.

Manpower And Skills Development

Most of the printers not originally retained from Trenton were hired in from other firms. Most printers had learned their skills in an informal way, undergoing a three-to-five year apprenticeship.

Entry level skills training was assigned to an OJT trainer on the floor who normally served as a printer. He was responsible for breaking in all new print personnel if production demands permitted. Otherwise, the new man was assigned to the printer. A similar procedure was followed in laminating-embossing, except that there was no trainer, and the man was assigned to the lead operator for training.

High turnover rates nullified these training efforts. The resulting falloff in production was threatening to management. Alpha had to hire and train replacements constantly because neither laminator-embossers nor print presses can be operated without full crews.

The plant environment had become severe. Management blamed the printers for the difficulty. The printers responded by insisting that they could not print quality goods with poor crews.

The falloff in productive efficiency, increases in lesser quality goods, high employee turnover and poor motivation, and the need for trained men were the factors which prompted Alpha to explore an upgrade program.

Chapters 3 and 4 of this report discuss the interests of the contractor in undertaking Alpha as an upgrade site.

Figure 2.1

ALPHA MANUFACTURING UNIT (SIMPLIFIED), ORGANIZATIONAL DIAGRAM*

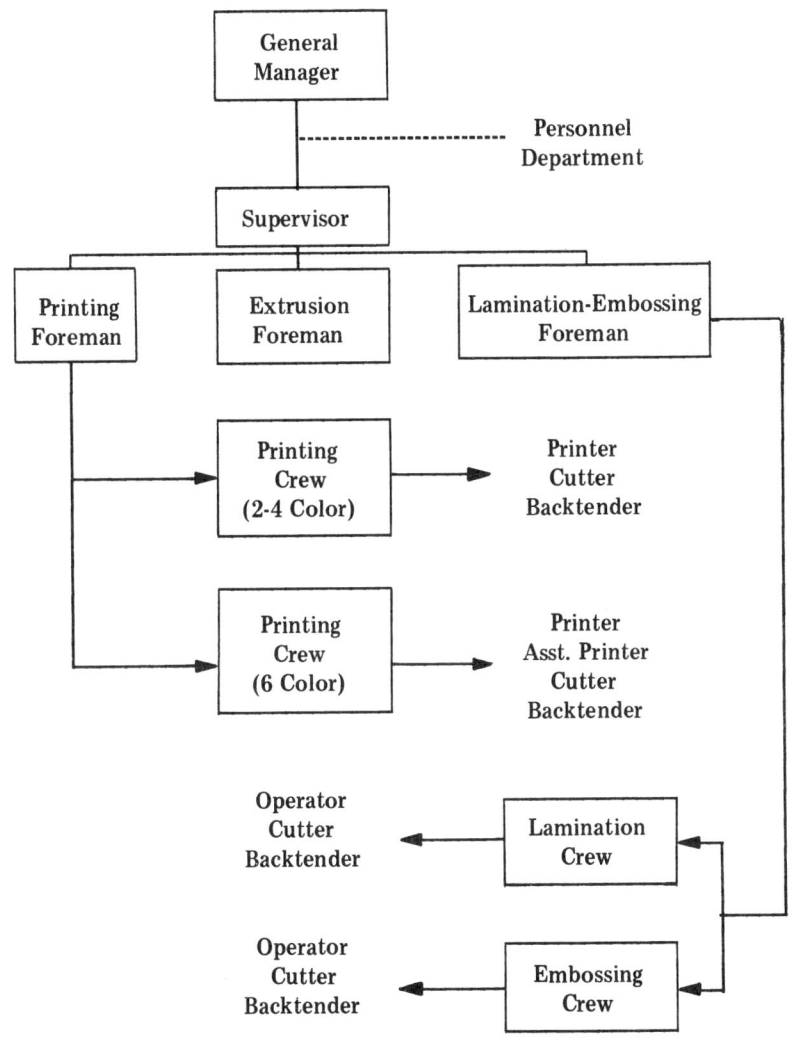

* A breakdown of Extrusion is excluded since no redesign was undertaken.

24

Figure 2.2
ALPHA PRODUCT FLOW (SIMPLIFIED)

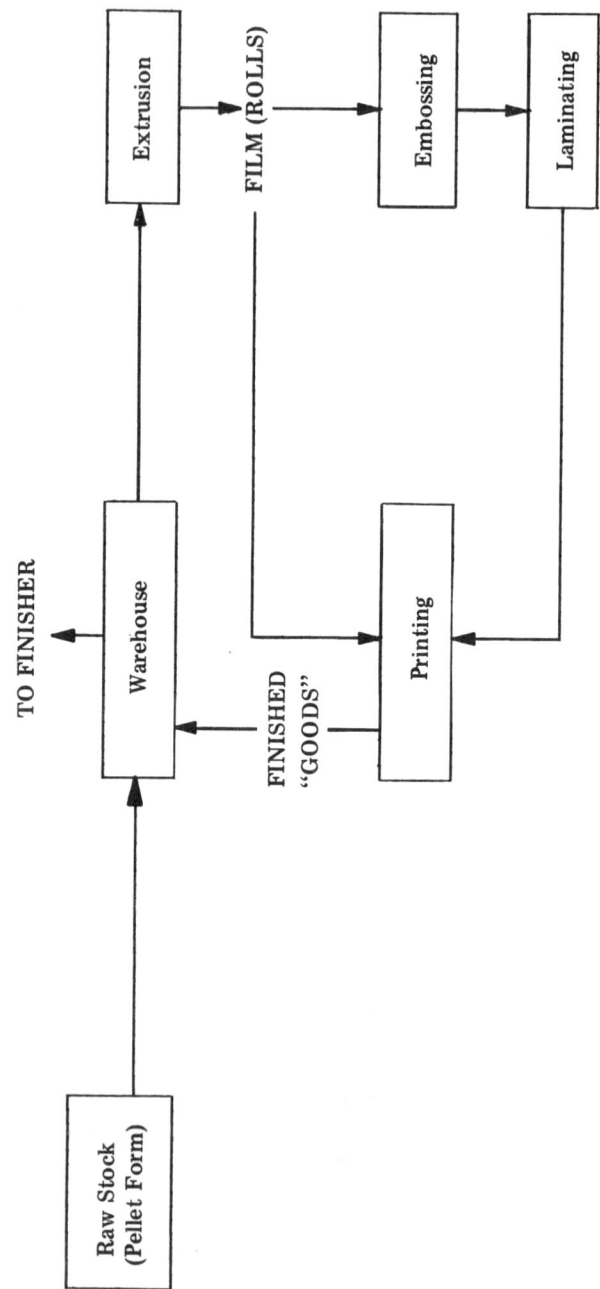

Table 2.1

UNEMPLOYMENT, BY CENSUS TRACTS
(Middlesex County)

Municipality	No. Males in Civilian Labor Force (1960)	Total (Male) Unemployment (1960)	% Unemployed
Edison	11,897	674	5.7
New Brunswick	11,091	1,006	9.1
Perth Amboy	11,205	1,036	9.2
Woodbridge	21,076	1,192	5.7
Carteret	5,838	365	6.3
Cranbury	630	12	1.9
Dunellen	2,007	103	5.1
East Brunswick	5,173	182	3.5
Highland Park	3,124	215	6.9
Jamesburg	799	66	8.3
Madison	5,742	241	4.2
Metuchen	3,798	144	3.8
Middlesex	1,559	62	4.0
Monroe Township	1,442	118	8.2
Middletown Borough	2,858	147	5.1
No. Brunswick	2,901	142	4.9
Piscataway Township	5,273	343	6.5
Plainsboro Township	385	12	3.1
South Amboy	2,346	143	6.1
So. Brunswick	2,785	112	4.0
Spotswood	1,755	69	3.9
So. Plainfield	4,795	250	5.2
South River	10,068	514	5.1
TOTAL	118,547	7,148	

Source: Figures through 1960 are from POPULATION TRENDS IN NEW JERSEY, RESEARCH REPORT NO. 123, Department of Conservation and Economic Development, State of New Jersey.

Table 2.2

ALPHA-UNION WAGE SCALE AT ENTRY AND AFTER ONE YEAR (1969-70)

INK. MANUF.	EXTRUSION	PRINTING	LAMINATION	EMBOSSING	WAREHOUSE
1 unit	3 units	6 units	2 units	2 units	1 unit
Operator ($82-90)	Lead Op. ($92-112)	Printer A ($140-220)	Operator ($90-106)	Operator ($90-106)	Ship-Rec. ($83-106)
Gen. Helper ($82-90)	Flat Die Op. ($88-106)	Printer B ($110-140)	Cutter ($82-90)	Cutter ($82-90)	Fork Lift ($82-90)
	Operator ($84-98)	Backtender ($82-90)	Backtender ($82-90)	Backtender ($82-88)	Packing ($82-88)
		Cutter ($82-88)			Gen. Helper ($82-88)

AUXILIARY

Pattern Maker ($90-110)	Ink Form ($90-106)	Maintenance A ($92-116)	Lab. Tech. ($90-116)	Copper Set-Up ($90-116)	Tube Insp. ($82-90)	Mill Op. ($82-102)
	Colorist ($90-106)	Maintenance B ($84-106)				

Table 2.3

ALPHA MANPOWER TURNOVER: ALL 1969 PRODUCTION
HIRINGS AND THEIR SEPARATIONS (6 MONTH FOLLOW-UP)

(Length of Service)

Production Area	1-3 Weeks	1 Month	2-3 Months	4-6 Months	Remaining Longer Than 6 Months	Total
Printing	48 (29%)	56 (34%)	26 (16%)	14 (9%)	19 (12%)	163 (100%)
Extruding	13 (19%)	21 (31%)	15 (22%)	6 (9%)	12 (18%)	67 (99%)
Laminating	20 (34%)	14 (24%)	9 (15%)	7 (12%)	9 (15%)	59 (100%)
	-------	-------	-------	-------	-------	-------
Total	81	91	50	27	40	289
Percent of Total	(28%)	(31%)	(17%)	(9%)	(14%)	(99%)
Cumulative Percent	(28%)	(59%)	(76%)	(85%)		

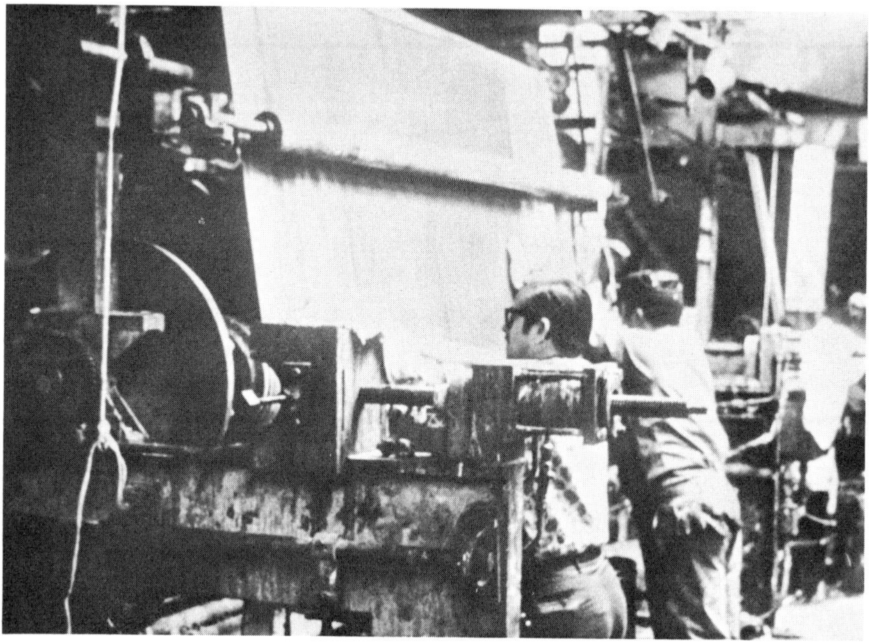

3

Upgrade Variables and Conditions

Company Site Selection

The selection of Alpha Plastics Printing Co., Inc. as an R & D site was conditioned by five main factors:

1. Verifying that the company did not have a systematic upgrading mechanism. It was experiencing problems of retention of its labor force at entry level and recruitment of workers at higher skilled printer levels.

2. Establishing that its problems could not be more directly resolved solely by having the company adjust its own entry level wage scale and/or competitively bidding for higher skilled employees on the open market.

3. Willingness of the company to experiment with a job redesign model and job progression ladder. If the planning and start-up was subsidized by the contractor, the company had to be willing to grant the wage increases earned by its upgraded employees.

4. Permitting the contractor, in return for providing certain resources, the opportunity to research and report out its findings.

5. Finally, receiving the sanction of the company and the union to conduct the project.

To establish this, the plant was visited and observed frequently; employees and company staff were interviewed, specific information from payroll was gathered, and the union contract was reviewed by the contractor.

Aside from the question of the specific type of upgrade model that might prove useful to Alpha (which the contractor was interested in researching), it is helpful to place the variables affecting upgrading in a specific company in the broader perspective of upgrade model development.

For continuity with other research efforts, a review of the main conditions and variables thought to have impact upon upgrading activities in industry was undertaken. The factors identified were extracted, added to and organized so as to structure a typological representation of the company.[1] Once derived, the typology permits the researcher to identify, codify and explicate the experience and research findings so that they are germane to the development of upgrade models. Where relevant to federal manpower policy, he must render these data pertinent.

Another purpose, in using a typological classification, is to better gauge which types of upgrading programs mesh with what types of industries and occupational fields.

Finally, a typology assists researchers to more generically identify conditions or variables affecting, not only the type of program, but institutional factors which may inhibit or promote upgrading on a continuing basis.

The specific parameters comprising the typology are defined and explained in Appendix A. The typology is subdivided into two main areas: Upgrading Conditions and Upgrade Climate.

1 Peter B. Doeringer & Michael J. Piore, INTERNAL LABOR MARKETS AND MANPOWER ANALYSIS, Lexington, Mass: Heath, 1971.

S. Brandwein, UPGRADING: PROGRAM EXPERIENCE AND POLICY CONSIDERATIONS, Department of Labor, 1971.

E. F. Shelley, CLIMBING THE JOB LADDER: A STUDY OF EMPLOYEE ADVANCEMENT IN ELEVEN INDUSTRIES; New York, 1970; UPGRADING THE WORK FORCE: PROBLEMS AND POSSIBILITIES, 1971.

Upgrade Conditions

The production facility and the products produced by Alpha are described in Chapter 2. We turn here to those factors which restrain or enhance job mobility within the plant itself.

Occupational Structure

The occupational structure of Alpha is typically shaped as a flat pyramid. Figure 2.1 illustrates the organization of job positions, and Table 2.2 lists the wages in all the major production areas

There was typically an operator or printer supported by a crew of two lesser skilled employees. The wage differential for lower skilled crew members was not markedly distinct, one from the other, or between production areas. There were two main categories: unskilled (general helpers, cutters and backtenders), earning between $82 and $90 per week, and skilled workers (printers, lamination, embossing, and extrusion operators), earning between $120 and $150 per week.

In addition, there were auxiliary craft jobs at Alpha. These jobs were filled, had virtually no turnover and, consequently, there was no possibility of upgrading to these positions in any large numbers. Planning for these positions was excluded from the scope of the project.

One foreman covered the print department, one covered lamination, and another, extrusion and embossing. These three foremen, in turn, were under a supervisor. This structure was maintained across all shifts. All reported to the General Manager, whose responsibility included both the New Brunswick and the Trenton plants.

Skilled/Unskilled Ratio

In printing, extrusion, laminating and embossing, the skilled/unskilled ratio was high; one skilled worker (printer or operator) for every two unskilled employees (cutter and backtender). This circumstance was viewed as favorable for upgrading, since any vacancy in printer or operator positions was a potential occasion for one of the two men in the crew to be upgraded (promoted).

Skills Differentiation

The skills differentiation between printer or operator and the rest of the crew was readily apparent, and generally was recognized within the plant. Briefly, printers were the most skilled, followed in turn by operators, and lastly by cutters and backtenders.

There was little in the way of skills to distinguish between cutters, whether they were in lamination, printing, extrusion or embossing. Similarly, backtenders were roughly uniform in skills when compared between departments. There were, however, some important distinctions between cutter and backtender, although primarily in printing, which are discussed in greater detail in the following chapter.

In summary, the skills differential was vertical within a department but only between the highest skill job (printer or operator) and the rest of the crew. Skills differences between departments were nil, excluding operator and printer differences. In fact, the position of general helper could be used as replacement for cutter or backtender in any department. Cutters could be interchanged between departments. It was even possible to move an employee from production to a warehouse assignment with no infringement of union contract job specification. (The reverse was not true because some skill training was required before a man could work as a cutter or backtender.)

Plant (Labor Force) Size

In terms of plant size, Alpha was considered a small plant. Excluding sales personnel, supervisory personnel, middle management and management, the labor force in production for three shifts was less than 90 employees.

In auxiliary (production) support functions, there were 22-23 men, and in warehouse (packing and shipping), between 20 and 40 men. The total blue collar labor force would fall between 132 and 163 men, say, 150 men on the average.

Table 3.1
Full Production Staffing Distributions

Production Area	3 Shifts	Backup	Total
Extrusion - Alpha	9	1	10
Printing - Alpha	38	3	41
- Trenton*	18	1	19
Laminating and Embossing	18	2	20
Total			90

* Included because of its relation to upgrading in computing promotion space.

At Alpha, three shifts were operated for printing, extrusion, and either laminating or embossing, whichever was needed. At Trenton, two presses were operated over three shifts, a laminator over two shifts.

Promotion Space

Promotion space delimited the number of higher skill job positions available: printer positions, operators in lamination and embossing, and lead operators in extrusion. In all three shifts, there were 33 potential upgrade positions. In reality, there were, of course, many fewer than 33 positions that could be filled. Only one vacancy existed in extrusion.[2] In lamination, there were four positions as operator open (3 actual, 1 backup), while in embossing all positions were filled. In print, each shift required a minimum of four printers. The third shift had three vacancies; absenteeism required two backup printers for the first and one for the second shift. Of the 9-12 print positions, turnover was estimated at 4-6 printers, resulting in a need

2 The upgrade program in extrusion was not carried out because of the limited number of positions available.

for 10+ new printers.[3] In sum, actual promotion space for program demonstration purposes was 10+ printers, 4 laminator operators, and 1 extrusion operator.[4]

Entry level jobs turned over at such a high rate that almost all new hires left employment within one year. While entry level training was not of central upgrade interest, in itself, it was focused on in order to enable employee-trainees to achieve print trainee status so they might subsequently become printers or operators. This applied only for the several cohorts of new hires who were to become printer or operator trainees. The turnover rates of these new employees was of special interest. It was assumed that an involvement in a company-sponsored upgrade program would result in greater employee commitment and thereby reduce turnover.

Upgrade Climate

Management Participation

In discussing managerial participation in upgrading, three levels of management need to be considered: (a) corporate management, (b) plant management, and (c) foremen and supervisors.

Contact with corporate management was maintained almost totally through the plant General Manager throughout the planning and operations period. While corporate management did not participate directly with the contractor, its views were interpreted and made known through the plant manager.

The plant General Manager was, to the contrary, extremely active in helping design, install, and promote the program. As a capable business man, he balanced the respective interests of the company, his own interest in having an in-house (plant) program, and the

---

[3] There was employee resentment about the absence of a complete replacement print crew so men could be relieved for lunch and time breaks. Responding to this need would have added two additional printers, although at the time of the program no such plan was agreed to.

[4] Fourteen printers were trained, anticipating program attrition. All successful trainee-employees were to receive their grade and wage even if more than 10 completed the program, and could not be placed on print machines. They would, in effect, be backup printers.

interests of the contractor in conducting an experimental upgrade program in industry.

The General Manager participated actively throughout the course of the study. There was no area which did not, at one time or another, require his intervention. He helped solve problems as they arose throughout the course of the project.

In describing upper management's role in the program, some of its attitudes are of importance in understanding the company. The company was generally suspicious of government-based projects. This "fear" appeared to be rooted in several factors:

1. The company's previous experience in applying for, and using, government funds was limited. Some OJT support provided under MDTA by the local State Employment Service was used to support the entry level training of four employees. The company was given the money, in front, and permitted to use it as it saw fit. The company had, it perceived, considerable latitude in using these OJT funds. The use of the funds was not reviewed and they were not penalized if the employee did not make the grade. The upgrade contract differed in that the company received a cost reimbursement for expenditures resulting from the program. In this, the company's expenditures were monitored, in that they were authorized only as they involved costs associated with the training of employees in its production facility. As a consequence, accountability was more stringent than it had experienced in the past.

2. The company expressed marked concern that the government would closely inspect its operations, fiscal structure (e.g., taxes), etc., because the contractor was funded by the government.

3. The company was concerned that it would be held "legally at fault" if it failed to promote employees, or if it wanted to get out of the program if it needed to. Its legal advisors reviewed the budget and the contractor's contract with the government. Since there was no formal contract between the government and the company this issue waned.

4. The company was concerned that the upgrade program would run it into debt, because of the necessity to initially hire larger numbers of employees at one time than was its usual practice (because of the need to build up a training group, cover employees on release time, and protect against turnover).

5. Of greatest concern was the question of the "cost to the company" in doing the program. They were also concerned about

increased seconds in print goods, lost production time as a result of release time, practice time on the machines, slower running speeds, wastage and potential damage to the copper print dies.

A sub-contract reimbursing the company for some of these items was provided as part of the program. The sub-contract estimates provided a small cushion to cover the possibility of excessive costs resulting from problems which might arise in the course of the project.

The existence of the sub-contract was to play a dual role in the course of the project. On the one hand, it was coveted by the company "as possibly some extra money"; on the other, as a "guarantee" that machines could be used for training, not solely for production. (Scheduling machines for training was always carefully scrutinized.)

Foremen and supervisors, while apprised of the project, never gave it their full support, nor did they believe the program would work. Even though several informing and planning sessions were jointly held at the beginning of the project, many of the operational difficulties encountered could be traced to their lack of support. (See Chapter 10 for a more detailed explanation.)

Plant Atmosphere and Attitudes

One should take into account the opinion that Alpha was a small company with a business-like, non-cosmopolitan regard for all of its employees. Management's view of upgrading was focused on entry level skills, and could be accurately characterized as wanting the entry level employee to "do his work well and not create any (work-discipline) problems." High turnover rates, frequent firings, employees quitting, and arguments over how much money should have been in the pay envelope were typical week-to-week occurrences.

Its concept of upgrading as well as its training experience was directed at entry level employees, breaking them in as backtenders, cutters, or general helpers, or failing that, letting the man go. (Under an MDTA-OJT contract for four employees, the training was the same as for their regular new hires. Off-site classes, educational inputs, and printer-oriented skills were never attempted before.)

Although two men had become printers, this occurred over the working life of the plant. That is, it took them over ten years to become printers.

Its view as to the difficulty of upgrading employees was not the same as regards lamination operators. It believed it was possible to upgrade such workers, but only over a long period of time.

All levels of management had reservations and doubts about an upgrade program directed toward developing printers. They never fully believed it was possible to upgrade the "typical" entry level employee into a fully qualified printer.

One company official, even though he actually advocated the upgrade program to the President as a partial solution to Alpha's production needs, said privately: "All I want and hope to get from you is three to four good printers. I don't think you can get any more than that. If you do it, I'll be happy. I don't believe you can get more than that."

Plant atmosphere for upgrading was poor but not unusual for low-wage firms. In part, concepts regarding upgrading were related to attitudes about the men who came to work at Alpha. The foremen and personnel officer were most skeptical about upgrading.

They recounted numerous experiences as to how men had failed to take advantage of their employment opportunities even when the company overextended its hand in support.

Foremen and employees frequently clashed around the question of rest, toilet, and lunch periods (men were required to eat their lunch at the print machine). Employees were challenged by the foremen whenever they were found away from their work station. The foremen did not believe there was a good reason for being discovered off the plant floor without permission. (Even heaters had been removed from the toilets so that men would not loiter there for a smoke.)

Composition of Labor Force

Middle management and management -- purchasing, sales, inventory control, and fiscal budgeting -- were white. All had been with the company for a long period of time. Clerical staff was composed of white females living within a 20 mile radius of the plant.

The production area (printing, lamination, embossing, and extrusion) in lower level skills was male, ethnically mixed (mainly Blacks, a few Puerto Ricans and whites). At higher skill levels (in production), the workers were ethnically mixed though mainly white. Foremen and supervisors were all white in printing; Black in lamination.

Some shift rotation did occur. More often than not, Blacks were on the third shift.

As noted, new hires were recruited from the local area (or were walk-ins). They were drawn from either the unemployed in the area or turnovers from other nearby plants. Higher skilled positions were mainly occupied by employees who had been with the company for some time, and had transferred to New Brunswick from Trenton.

Employee Participants

The upgrade plan involved, to varying degrees, several levels of employee participants. First, at entry level, all new hires were hired on a "first-come, first-serve" basis. They were hired as they could be fitted into the training cycle schedules. Later, after training, a number of new hires were moved into higher skill positions. Second, presently-employed mid-level workers were trained for higher skills and job promotions as printers or operators. Third, OJT trainers were developed, taken from Alpha's print and lamination departments, with a view to their promotion to permanent status as trainers or as A printers.

Type of Production

Perhaps one of the most critical structural factors was the type of productive organization. As mentioned earlier, Alpha printed plastics in roll form on high-speed print machines, the type of production classified in the typology as crew-machine. The basic crew (printing) consisted of a cutter, backtender, and printer. (In addition, there was a foreman who checked the operation of all presses.)

The cutter, one of the unskilled members of the crew, was stationed at the output side of the press. His function was to monitor the flow and quality of the print product and to cut off completed goods to specific yardage. It generally took Alpha two to four weeks to train a cutter to proficiency. In this period, he also learned about the variety of printed plastics and how to handle each. This was an entry level position.

The backtender, stationed at the input side of the press, fed materials to the press, supplied ink as needed, and checked on the movement of materials through the press. It generally took Alpha from four to six weeks to train a backtender. This was also an entry level position although more difficult than that of the cutter.

The highest position within the print crew was occupied by the printer. He had over-all responsibility for directing the activities of the cutter and backtender. He was responsible for the quality of the product, including accurate register, press speed, etc. The printer was the most skilled member of the crew. As reported, it took about three years or more to train a good printer, and the market for printers was reported to be highly competitive

A similar form of crew-machine productive organization existed for laminators. The laminator (operator) performed many of the same functions as the printer, except the work was much less complex because of its lesser complexity as a machine compared to the print presses.

The type of production largely determined the decision to field a job redesign upgrade model. The presses, as pointed out earlier, largely determined the physical position of each man in the crew, how much and what he had to do, and the amount of time in which he had to do it. Unless there was some redesign of the duties around the press, it would not be readily possible to permit men to learn the print trade while they were on the job. (This issue is discussed in greater detail in Chapter 4.)

Union Local 1200

The union local at Alpha Plastics was part of a larger international union covering employees in another, not directly related industry (electrical workers). Local 1200 represented Alpha employees. The international had several other locals in the New Brunswick area in plants directly related to its prime industrial focus.

The contract between Alpha and Local 1200 served as a main guideline for employee-management disputes, supplemented by precedents and informal agreements. The union representative, Ralph, was a Black man who had been with the company for many years. He had been a production worker. Upon his election by the union membership, he moved to a new position as mail clerk affording more time for him to carry out union business.

Ralph served as the main interpreter of the contract for employees who thought they had a grievance; he would carry the union position into meetings with management. In general, clear violations of company policy resulted in the employee's termination. Except for cases where the employee was an "old timer" with a good record, employees were dismissed outright without review by the Personal Department which, on paper, had sole authority for firing employees. This unit of management was vested with the sole right to hear appeals.

Some five years earlier, Ralph was almost removed as the union representative. However, there was no one in the membership who came forth as a candidate. Union meetings, employees complained, were rarely held. When they were, they were multi-plant, wherein the issues and complaints of any one plant were passed over in the general discussion or tabled for the next meeting. One employee remarked: "We don't know what's going to be discussed, except everyone will say something and we won't get anything settled or decided. There are too many guys, and we don't get to stay with our situation at Alpha."

Contract renewals were, by way of contrast, bargaining sessions that went down to the contract expiration deadline. One company official said: "There is hard bargaining, but the whole thing could really be settled earlier. I think there would be some criticism if we didn't go to the end."

Alpha had been able to avoid a strike over the years. Given Alpha's fiscal operating margin and productive ability, it is probable that a protracted strike at any time would have severely crippled Alpha and caused bankruptcy.

Union Procedure and Participation

Union participation in the formation and conduct of the upgrade program was supportive. It was receptive to the program and would not place any barriers in the way of the program as long as its membership was fairly treated, e.g., seniority rules would be observed and its members could participate and get promoted. In effect, the union role was to remain passive and non-hostile to the program. As the union representative indicated, the concept of an upgrading program meshed with the desire of the union to improve the status of its membership. Consequently, no opposition at all was encountered.

Management took the lead in informing and describing the program at a joint meeting attended by the State (regional) representative of the union, Ralph, and the contractor. (The President of the local had already been informed of the project, and had given his approval.)

The discussion centered around three main topics: (a) the mutual interest of the company and union in improving the status of the employees, (b) the importance of the educational components of the proposed upgrade plan, and (c) the feeling that the present membership had always wanted and asked for education and training and that all employees coming to Alpha should get the same benefits.

At a subsequent meeting, which included Ralph, two active union members and one of the OJT trainers, these specifics were reviewed. No issues emerged around the question of seniority. Those questions which did emerge related to eligibility in participating in the program (open to all employees, senior employees and new hires), whether the company would upgrade the successful trainee (at what wage rate), and what would the company do if everyone passed.

The discussions moved to the question of organizational liaison. Subsequently, the upgrade program was placed under the aegis of the union's Welfare and Benefits Committee.

In the months that followed, the union did assist in trying to get present employees to participate in the program; did act to "protect" new hires (once union members) when in conflict with supervisory personnel (less so after the contractor completed its work and left Alpha); did not restrict new hires from becoming union members after 30 days; and posed no objections to both new and senior employees being upgraded.

No further meetings evolved. It was not considered necessary by the union, even though there was a concerted attempt on the part of the contractor to have the union participate fully and openly in the design and management of the project. (See Chapter 10 for a summary evaluation and judgment of the union's role.)

Upgrade Criteria

Prior to the current project, promotion to printer almost never occurred through in-plant upgrading. Most printers were hired in.

Upgrade criteria, for program purposes, posed no major obstacle. Careful interpretation of the seniority rules was important. All job positions were acquired, first, by seniority; and second, by skill. Thus, if there was to be a hiring for the printer position, it was posted and bid. If the employee had the skill, he was eligible for selection by seniority. The contract on this issue read, as follows:

Article VI - Promotion

Section 1 - Promotion is defined as the transfer of an employee from one job classification in which the wage rate is higher. In all cases of promotion of employees the following factors shall be considered by the Company: (a) Length of continuous service; (b) Knowledge, training, ability, skill, efficiency; (c) Physical fitness; and (d) Attendance record.

Where factors (b), (c) and (d) are relatively equal, the length of continuous service shall govern.

Section 2 - New openings shall be posted on the bulletin board for a period of five (5) days before being filled.

Section 3 - No employee receiving equivalent pay in one category may post for a job of the same pay in another category.

Alpha had no formal training procedure or capability. By contract, it had license to hire outsiders if it did not find these skills among its present employees.

Several consequences follow:

1. If the present employee was senior to another employee, but did not have the requisite skills, the junior employee, trained for printer (for example), might be selected.

2. For new hires, once they had become union members, the same rule applied. For example, if a senior employee and a new hire (union member) were equally skilled for a print position, the senior employee would be upgraded first. If there were more openings, then a new man might be upgraded even if he was junior in seniority to other present employees, provided he had the skills and they didn't.

3. In the context of a training program to fill a large number of openings, the essential non-contractual but programmatic requirement was that the senior employee be given first opportunity to participate

in the program, that he not be excluded by a new hire. Both the new hire and senior employee could join the upgrade program. In these instances, it was not important whether or not the new employee was a union member at the outset. It was essential that the opportunity for receiving skills training was made available to both senior and junior employees, including new hires who would become union members without restriction after 30 days.

Present Upgrade Practices

Historically, Alpha filled printing positions from the outside, hiring in experienced men. (Only two men ever worked up to printer at Alpha.) For this type of industry, it was commonplace to raid other manufacturers to secure good printers. (Some firms had gentlemen's agreements to curtail reciprocal raiding.)

Lamination operators were also hired from the outside, but there was a history of some men working up into operator.

Company Training Capability

Alpha had no formal training capability. There was no training department or separate training staff. No formal printer or operator training had previously been attempted.

New men had to be trained as cutters, backtenders, or general helpers. The method consisted either of showing the general helper what to do on the floor or, for cutters and backtenders, assigning a man to train them. The OJT trainer was, when not training, a printer. The man was carefully shown what to do; machines were slowed so he could practice cutting. Thereafter, he was assigned to the regular printer, who continued to "break him in."

The man usually proved out in two to four weeks.

Upgrade Job Positions

The data on promotion space indicated need for printers mainly and lamination operators secondarily. (The contractor could not field a program for the one extrusion operator; no training in this area occurred.)

Upgrade Skill Levels

The skill level of the printer exceeded all other production workers. The skill level of printers was initially estimated by reviewing their educational backgrounds and skill training. Most had completed high school (usually vocational school), and afterwards had "apprenticed" themselves to printers who taught them the skill. It took somewhere between three to five years before they were able to prove out and get their own printing assignment.

Paraphrasing an interview with one of the Alpha printers helped to round out the picture.

> The machines could be learned if someone showed you what to do and when to do it. But you really need a lot of practice to get it under your belt, and you need to know the principles beside the dials. All machines are different. You get to know a machine and when it feels or sounds wrong and what to do.
>
> I guess I could handle one of the other machines; I don't know. I think I could only teach a man on this machine, if he really wanted to learn it, and would stay with it. But you know, not everybody can learn. It depends on the individual.

Lamination operators performed similar work tasks as printers, but the job was easier because of the absence of color printing and color registry. The machines were simpler to operate relative to the printing presses.

Lamination operators had completed or almost completed regular or vocational high school. Most learned the job by working in a plant that laminated, and then came to Alpha; some learned lamination at Alpha, taking somewhere between 7 to 10 years before they got a laminating assignment.

Company Reasons for Participating

Multiple reasons were responsible for Alpha's interest and decision to participate in the upgrade program. For purposes of analysis, it is important to distinguish between *primary* and *supporting* reasons for participating and those elements that did not constrain against an affirmative decision. The primary factors have already been described, but are nonetheless summarized below.

1. *Primary Factors:*

   a. Desire to stop and to then reverse the slippage in production;

   b. Skill shortages;

   c. Poor quality of workmanship, especially in attaining first quality goods; and

   d. High turnover.

2. *Supporting Factors:*

   a. Poor worker discipline ascribed by the company to entry level employees;

   b. Employee pressures arising from discontent with working conditions; and

   c. Dissatisfaction of present skilled employee in not being able to earn incentive bonuses because of low productivity.

3. *Decision Factors:* While upper management had reservations about upgrading the "typical" entry level employee as far as printer, it decided in favor of the program because of its belief that the program could produce results in addressing the issues identified above, for the reason that:

   a. Entry level employees would be better trained;

   b. Some printers would likely be developed, at least from senior employees;

   c. Participation with an outside contractor would not be costly;

   d. Participation would not subject the company to government intrusion, red tape or inspection;

   e. Agreement and support could be had of operational staff and the union; and

   f. No constraint on the company would obtain to upgrade in terms of its contractual agreements with the union.

Summary

Factors that affect upgrade potential within a company are identified and are seen to be complexly related to structural variables and conditions, as well as to the climate of a company. This discussion serves to set the stage for a more detailed analysis of how these factors operated in producing the observed results of this demonstration. Table 3.2 outlines the typographical features found at Alpha.

Table 3.2

TYPOLOGICAL REPRESENTATION
ALPHA PLASTICS PRINTING CO., INC.

I. UPGRADE CONDITIONS

Classification	Rating	Remarks	Classification	Rating	Remarks
Occupational Structure			**Promotion Space**		
a) Long, narrow pyramid			a) High (40+)		
b) Moderate pyramid			b) Moderate (10+)	X	
c) Flat pyramid	X		c) Low (1-10)		
d) Craft, trades					
Skilled/Unskilled Employee Ratio			**Skills Differentiation**		
a) High	X		a) High	X	High in vertical line, low in horizontal, e.g., between departments.
b) Moderate			b) Low		
c) Low					
Plant (Labor Force) Size					
a) Large					
b) Moderate					
c) Small	X				

Table 3.2 (Cont'd)

TYPOLOGICAL REPRESENTATION
ALPHA PLASTICS PRINTING CO., INC.

II. UPGRADE CLIMATE

Classification	Rating	Remarks	Classification	Rating	Remarks
Production Management			**Type of Training**		
a) Active	X		a) Classroom		
b) Limited			b) Supervisory training		
			c) Formal OJT		
			d) Experience-on-job	X	
First Line Supervisory			**Employee-Trainees**		
a) Active	X		a) Employed, low (poverty) income		
b) Limited			b) Unemployed	X	
			c) Racial minorities		
			d) Middle-level employees	X	
Union Interest			**Type of Production Organization**		
a) Continuous interest			a) Assembly line		
b) Focal interest	X		b) Man-machine		
			c) Crew-machine	X	
Selection Criteria: Upgrade			d) Craft		
a) Seniority-bidding	X				
b) Open-bidding	X				
c) Hiring-in					

Table 3.2 (Cont'd)

TYPOLOGICAL REPRESENTATION
ALPHA PLASTICS PRINTING CO., INC.

II. UPGRADE CLIMATE (Cont'd)

Classification	Rating	Remarks
Type of Upgrading		
a) New hires (entry level)..............	X	
b) Entry level to middle level.........	X	
c) Middle level to higher skill.........	X	
d) Higher skill to supervisory		
e) Supervisory to middle management		

Classification	Rating	Remarks
Industry Goals		
a) Turnover and absenteeism............	X	
b) Poor quality of workmanship........	X	
c) Poor worker discipline		
d) Skill shortages...........	X	
e) Desire to increase production........	X	
f) Technological changes		
g) Union pressure		
h) Employee pressure		

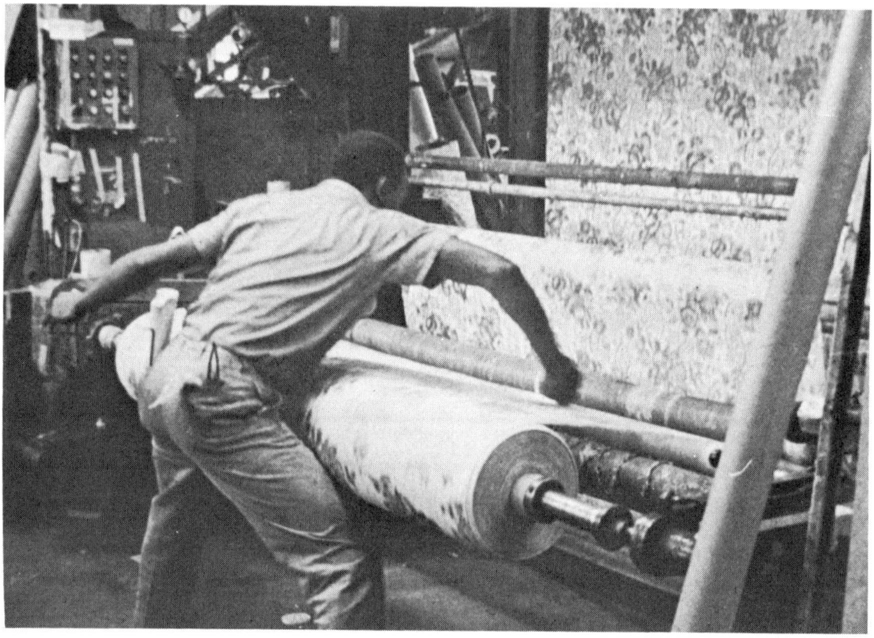

4
Job Redesign and Job Ladder Development

A major objective of the program was to demonstrate the utility of industry-focused techniques in the development of skilled manpower. In Alpha's case, some form of job redesign was necessary (see Chapter 2). This had to be directed toward rapidly producing printers and operators, with a minimal strain on the company's method of organizing production.

The job redesign had to meet several specifications because of the company's specific methods of production:

1. The duties and responsibilities of each crew member's work station needed to be changed because each man was physically separated, one from the other, and there was no way in which higher skills learning could take place while working at only one job station.

2. The newly designed job stations had to be supportable by training (either vestibule or formal OJT), provided by separate staff, because the printer was not sufficiently free from his duties to provide total apprenticeship training.

3. For the employee-trainee, further apprenticeship and seasoning would also need to occur, but only after his assignment as a printer (or operator), not before.

4. The job redesign had to "protect" Alpha's almost automatic, very rapid crew-machine production; otherwise, the company would find the costs of training prohibitive. The machines could not be slowed for prolonged periods or left idle to satisfy training needs. The redesign had to blend in with Alpha's routine operating procedures.

Redesigning Printer Jobs

The primary data for the job redesign was obtained from a job task analysis (JTA) of the work duties and skills requirements of all job positions involved in the upgrade program. (The JTA analyses are described in detail in Appendix D.)

A key element in this job redesign was the interfacing of the cutter and backtender job with those job functions performed by the printer or operator (in laminating-embossing). A method was sought which would enable the lower skilled employees to learn some of the higher skilled job functions while working as a cutter or backtender.

The method required that the printer's job be analyzed (using JTA). Starting with his receipt of the print order, all aspects of the job were observed: set-up and start-up, regulation of input and output controls, tending and quality control. These skill components of the printer's job were observed over several different types of product runs.

To provide for those printer job functions which could be learned while working as a cutter or backtender, the observed job tasks were broadly divided into two related, though separable job components:

1. Press setup and tending, including input and output duties, and
2. Press control, monitoring and quality product methods (requiring print theory and knowledge of control procedures).

The first job component was less dependent upon learning the principles and theory of printing than the latter component. The redesign required the printer to "step back" somewhat, to allow some of his job duties (the first component) to be reassigned to the cutter-backtender as part of the "redesigned job" (see Figure 4.1). The second component was "reserved" as a requisite for the print trainee.

This allowed for greater quality control. For example, the printer, because he was "freed" from some duties, could now allocate more of his time to the scheduling and inspection of goods sent to his department.

One dividend of this redesign was that it permitted the cutter-backtender to learn one major part of the printer's job by having him actually take over the performance of it. Another dividend occurred later in the program when the cutter-backtender was assigned as a trainee to the print station. This enabled the printer or OJT trainer to instruct the trainee specifically on the more skilled aspects of the printer's job. (The instructor could assume that the trainee already knew many of the basics.)

Redesigning Cutter and Backtender Jobs

A similar method was utilized in redesigning the lower-skilled jobs, but along differing principles. In the past, a new man was first assigned as a backtender on the basis that the printer or operator could help him to learn the job since they were physically nearer to him by virtue of their job station at the press. As a consequence of the JTA, it was determined that the backtender's job was the more difficult compared to that of the cutter. In addition to the functions of having to mount and splice goods, the backtender was responsible for maintaining ink in the nips and for centering goods on the blanket (border control). It took three to four weeks to learn the job.

Exempting his quality control responsibility, the cutter was mainly required to cut goods from the running web, semi-automatically attaching the tail to the new core through the use of a rewind machine. This skill could be learned quickly, granting the fact that the speed and reflexes needed to permit him to cut and meet production standards might take longer. However, this relatively easier job was held by the more experienced man in the crew because of the need to place the new man at the backtender station so he could be observed by the printer.

The job duties of both the cutter and the backtender were similar, i.e., in cutting and in shared duties when changing over to run new goods. Both were readily amenable to rapid training. As a consequence,

Figure 4.1
JOB REDESIGN, CUTTER & BACKTENDER
I. Work Stations (Before Redesign)

Skills Inventory

Job Title	"Beginner"	"Experienced" Man

Cutter	A. TENDING
	  1. Operates rewind stand and cuts from running roll.
	  2. Resets all counters.
	  3. Adjusts tension for new roll.
	B. OFFBEARING:
	  Moves roll from rewind stand to pallet.
	C. FEEDING:
	  Mounts new core on rewind stand.
		D. QUALITY CONTROL:
		  Reports all foldovers, smears, registration faults to printer. Detects and reports other faults such as blocking or marking-off.
		E. HANDLING:
		  During setup & breakdown:
		  1. Brings coppers to press.
		  2. Delivers ink.
		  3. Makes and positions dams and plugs.
		  4. Webs the press.
		  5. Positions doctor blade.
		  6. Makes and positions flag (sample).
		  7. Removes old copper and mounts new.

Backtender	F. COPYING:
	  Records yardage for each roll fed to machine.
	G. HANDLING:
	  Mounts new rolls and tapes film to running web on time.
		H. COMPARING:
		  Checks label on raw film against dye order.
		I. COMPUTING:
		  Computes total yardage for each color & totals against dye order.
		J. TENDING:
		  1. Controls ink pump.
		  2. Maintains nip for each color.
		  3. Adds solvent to ink
		K. CONTROLLING:
		  1. Maintains border.
		  2. Reports all faults to printer.
		L. HANDLING:
		  (Same as "E".)

Figure 4.1 (Cont'd)

II. Redesigned Work Stations

CUTTER-BACKTENDER

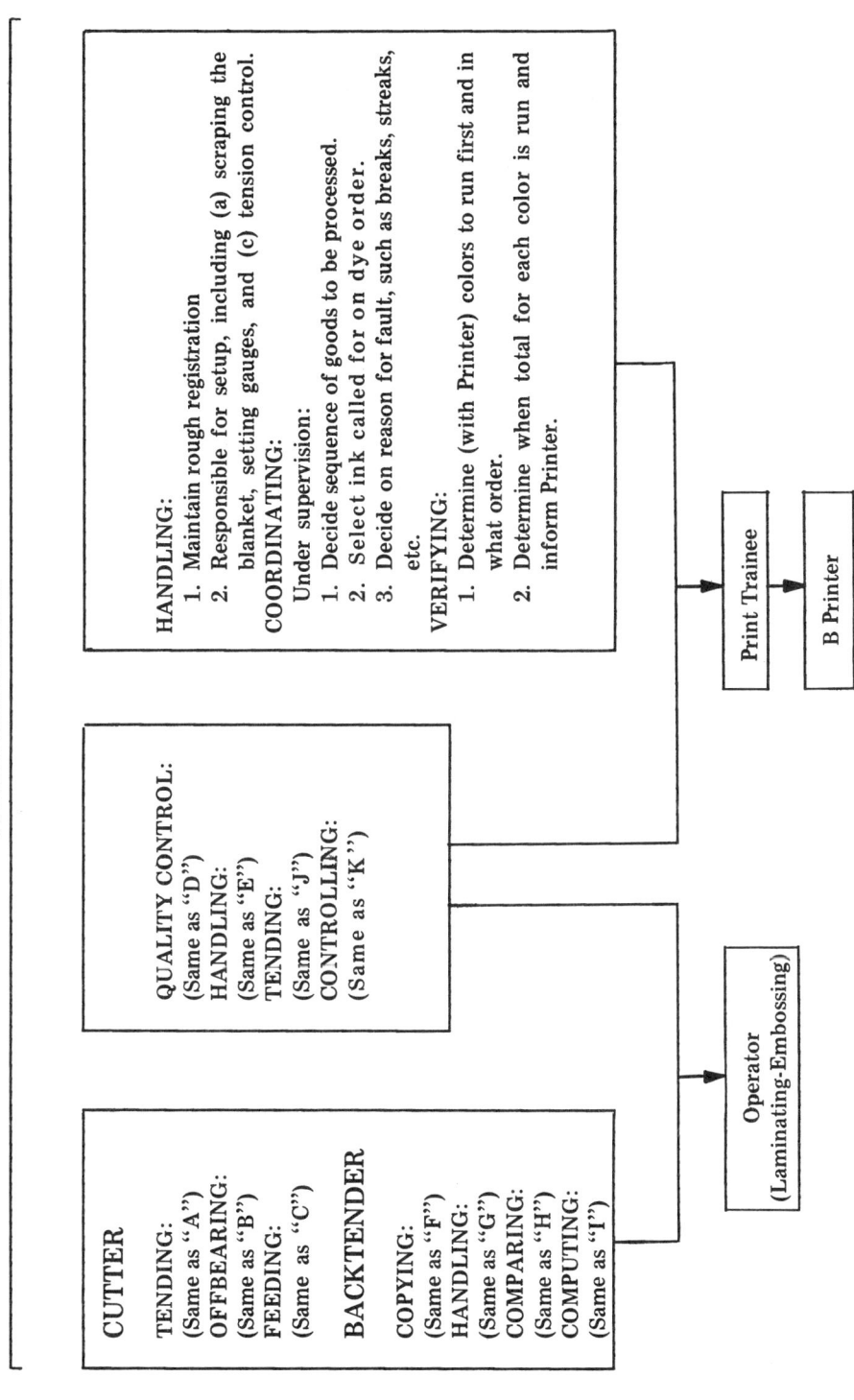

CUTTER

TENDING:
(Same as "A")
OFFBEARING:
(Same as "B")
FEEDING:
(Same as "C")

BACKTENDER

COPYING:
(Same as "F")
HANDLING:
(Same as "G")
COMPARING:
(Same as "H")
COMPUTING:
(Same as "I")

→ Operator (Laminating-Embossing)

QUALITY CONTROL:
(Same as "D")
HANDLING:
(Same as "E")
TENDING:
(Same as "J")
CONTROLLING:
(Same as "K")

HANDLING:
1. Maintain rough registration
2. Responsible for setup, including (a) scraping the blanket, setting gauges, and (c) tension control.

COORDINATING:
Under supervision:
1. Decide sequence of goods to be processed.
2. Select ink called for or on dye order.
3. Decide on reason for fault, such as breaks, streaks, etc.

VERIFYING:
1. Determine (with Printer) colors to run first and in what order.
2. Determine when total for each color is run and inform Printer.

→ Print Trainee

→ B Printer

55

the job of cutter and backtender could be merged together into a new job called cutter-backtender.

The job of cutter-backtender was divided into three job components:

1. Those basic elements which "protected production" (e.g., in cutting without waste), and quality control.

2. Those tending operations which were necessary to maintaining the operation of the press: ink mixing and supply, tending and replacement of rollers and worn parts, and materials supply.

3. Those first-level printer functions which were added to the job of cutter-backtender (formerly assigned to the printer), now reassigned as part of the "redesigned job" to be performed during setup and breakdown by all members of the crew.

The new employee was expected to learn the basic job fairly quickly. As he became more experienced, he could also learn (in class) how to tend and to take over the first level printing functions. During the work assignments of tending, setup and breakdown, the cutter-backtender could continue to learn what the printer did and why he did it.

As a print trainee, he could learn the theory and the more complex aspects of press control, monitoring and quality product methods. After these aspects of the printer's job were learned, he could be assigned to the printer's station to work with the OJT trainer to learn the balance of the printer's job.

Among the advantages of this redesign model were the protective elements (e.g., reducing wastage) which could be taught immediately to all new employees. Another advantage was that either the cutter or the backtender, now one and the same, could manage each other's job station. Both were available to perform the "redesigned job," as a beginning step in their experience as a print trainee.

Certifying the New Jobs

The cutter-backtender job was also an interim step while the employee trained to become a printer. The cutter-backtender job, because it was created out of two existing job titles, did require union-management consent as to title, job duties and wage scale even though

Job Redesign And Job Ladder Development

it was not a job title enumerated within the company's labor contract. There were no recognized trainee positions in the union contract.

Neither company nor union approval for the job title of print trainee was required, because it was possible to utilize an existing job title while modifying the duties for training purposes. Alpha had three printer positions listed in their union contract: (a) Assistant Printer, (b) B Printer, and (c) A Printer. The A printer job position was the most skilled; and the assistant printer title was reserved for the beginning printer who qualified in skills ability but did not have requisite experience. In analyzing the various printer's functions, the basic difference between assistant printer and the B printer was identified as being essentially one of responsibility and experience rather than job skill.

As a consequence, it was possible to designate the print trainee job as a position already recognized by contract because of its relative similarity to the job of the assistant printer. (The full title and grade of assistant printer could not be used because of the large number of trainees who were performing as print trainees.)

The employee training for printer "occupied" the assistant printer position as one part of his training and as a cutter-backtender in performing his normal work (non-training) duties. Thus, during a typical week the print trainee wore two hats. When not assigned as a print trainee (three days per week), he worked as a cutter-backtender. When assigned to print training (two days per week), he spent four hours during each of two days in the classroom; and four hours, working on the print press with an instructor in *formal* OJT. When receiving OJT or practice experience, the print trainee was assigned to a print crew as a supernumerary (he became the fourth member of a three-man crew). Under the printer's command, he did some of the printer's work, such as ink mixing, color registry, and so on. It provided the print trainee with the beginning fundamentals, those necessary to understanding the operation of the press with the least disruption in production. In effect, the skills learned were staged so that the print trainee was able to perform all the tasks necessary to sustain production, while at the same time he was learning to understand the more difficult operations of the press. As such, he was given progressive responsibilities for operation of the press (replacing the printer).

The final test of the print trainee's ability to function independently was his demonstrated ability to operate a 2-color press while supervising a crew of two other men for a period of two weeks (on his own). He could, of course, call upon the printer, the print foreman, and the trainer to help him resolve the problems he encountered.

This final step in his training was called the "solo trial period." On successful completion, he was to be graduated with the title of B printer

Job Ladders

Print Department

Of the four print machines in New Brunswick, one printed 2-colors, two printed 3- or 4-colors and one printed 6-colors. The 6-color press was manned by a crew of four men, and only here an assistant printer was assigned (4-crew press). In point of fact, the larger press was generally manned by an A and B printer, there being only one assistant printer on the entire Alpha staff.

Ignoring the assistant printer title, the career ladder designed for the print department, from simple to the most complex, was as follows:

Revised (New) Job Ladder

1 - Cutter-backtender

2 - Print Trainee

3 - B Printer

4 - A Printer

In comparison, the following job progressions existed at Alpha previously:

Old Job Ladder

1 - General Helper
  (assigned as Backtender)[1]
2 - Backtender
3 - Cutter
4 - B Printer
5 - A Printer

The effect of the redesign -- the new job ladder -- was to establish a position, one of cutter-backtender, the gap between this job and that of printer to be filled by a newly designated job (during training only) of Print trainee.

Laminating-Embossing Department

The two laminators were run by a crew of four; the embossers, by a crew of three. The cutter-backtender job was the only job in this department which required redesign. Following this redesign, the progression, from simple to the most complex, was as follows:

Revised (New) Job Ladder

Embossing	Lamination
1 - Cutter-backtender	1 - General Helper
2 - Operator	2 - Cutter-backtender
	3 - Operator

---

[1] Alpha had employed the title of General Helper because its union contract permitted them to assign such a worker to a multitude of jobs, including such assignments as general helper (on the floor), janitor, warehouseman, etc. More importantly, this title was employed to enable Alpha to move men from job-to-job in the print department as crews needed to be filled and presses started to avoid seriously affecting production resulting from turnover and absences. In fact, a machine could not be started unless it had a crew of 3 or 4 men depending on its size.

In comparison, the following job progression existed at Alpha previously:

Old Job Ladder

Embossing	Lamination
1 - Backtender	1 - General Helper
2 - Cutter	2 - Backtender
3 - Operator	3 - Cutter
	4 - Operator

In changing the jobs in laminating-embossing, only the cutter and backtender jobs were redesigned. The job of cutter-backtender was similar in almost every regard to the job performed in the print department.

The operator's job was not changed because the design of the equipment allowed the operator to run the machine at a slower rate of speed. As well, the number of controls was limited. The most difficult part of the job was restricted to setup. Here the supervisor could be of direct help in making sure the job met specification before it was run.

Wage Scales

The hiring rate was $84 per week ($2.10 per hour). Upon completion of cutter-backtender training, the wage scale was raised to $90 per week ($2.25 per hour). On becoming a print trainee or operator, the employee earned $110 per week ($2.75 per hour).

Completion of print training, after successful completion of his two-week solo demonstration, entitled the employee to a wage raise to $140 per week ($3.50 per hour) and the grade of B printer. (Progress to A printer was to occur over time as the employee picked up additional experience and seasoning while working as a B printer.)

Summary

In the job redesign, a "new" job was created, in part from two separate jobs (because of their similarities), in part from the higher skill job. The employee-trainee could learn and practice some of the advanced skills as part of his new job duties.

A progression ladder was structured which differed from the old job ladder. The creation of the new job ladder (and the new job) did not require union-management sanction because of its similarity to a rarely used job position. In effect, the redesign restructured the duties for an existent title. As a last step, wage scale adjustments were determined in line with the new structure. These were made dependent on the employee-trainee's progress as he moved up the ladder.

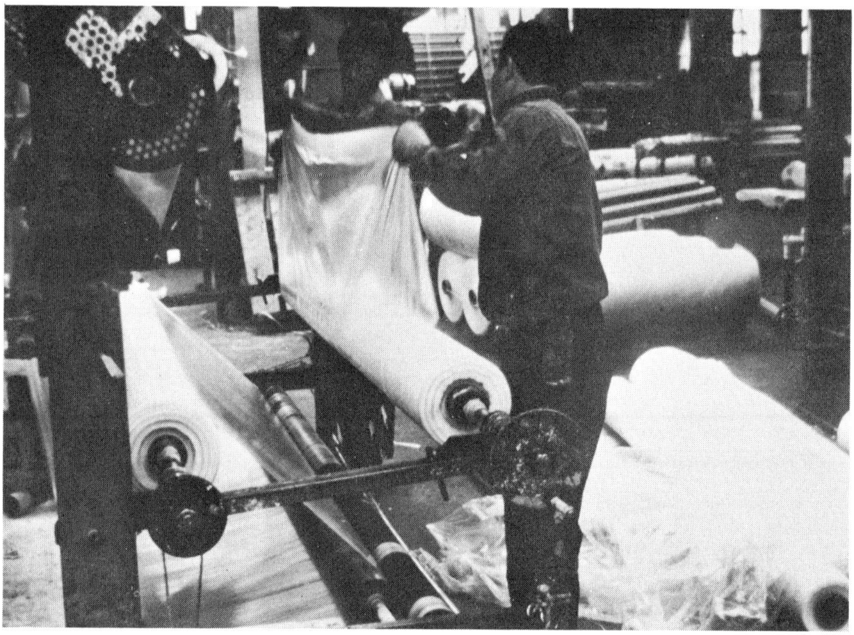

5

Program Parameters

Recruitment and Hiring

Alpha interviewed all new applicants, made its selection, and hired the men. Alpha's intrinsically high turnover rate, anticipated program attrition, and the need to fill a training-cycle class required hiring more employees, at one time, than was Alpha's usual practice. The company was more selective in seeking men who would be willing to go into the program. It held open some non-production jobs for men who were good workers but who dropped out of the program (separations from the training program did not require the employee to leave the company). More typically, an employee would have a grievance with the company that led to his quitting or being fired, resulting in his separation from the program as well.

The resources available, the length of time required to complete a printer-training cycle, limited the number of such cycles. It was necessary to build up sufficient class size ($N = 8$ minimum) to initiate each new cycle. In order to bring more employees into Alpha, a more intensive recruiting effort was undertaken, utilizing advertisements in the local newspaper and referrals from public agencies in the area. The recruitment effort had to be sustained, but the response was sufficient to bring applicants to the company.

The hiring policy at the company, even prior to the program, was not restrictive (except as noted below). If the man was judged physically able and expressed a willingness to work he was hired, provided language was not a handicap. (This tended to exclude some foreign-born and Puerto Rican applicants.) If the applicant looked like a hippie or was thought to be on drugs, he was screened out by Alpha's Personnel Officer.

On completion of its regular hiring procedure, the company routed the new employee to the contractor. He was interviewed and tested, and barring any reading difficulties, asked if he would like to participate in the upgrade program.

Except for two restrictions, all employees were taken on a "first come, first serve" basis. First, a man who was color blind was not permitted to enter the print training program, since color discrimination was a prerequisite of quality control. He could, however, enter the program for lamination operator and/or the GED program. Second, a man who, upon testing, was unable to read (i.e., fell below 6th grade in paragraph meaning on the Stanford Achievement Test) was not allowed to enter the GED program. The education program was not designed to be used with those who were functionally illiterate.[1] The expectation was that he would be referred to a community-based Adult Basic Education program. In practice, no such program was active in the community and, consequently, only tutoring was provided by the project staff. He was not prohibited from joining the first phase of the skills training program (cutter-backtender). He could not enter print or operator training since he would not be able to use the instruction manual. Three employees were rejected on this basis.

[1] Some employees scoring just below 6th grade were taken into the GED program; none below fourth grade (see Appendix C).

It was thought that these candidates would benefit from the instruction in reading comprehension and mathematics. They had not been in school for some time. The assumption was made that stimulation of their academic interests would result in sufficient improvement so as to permit their entry into the full GED program. They were retested later in the program for reading growth. In many instances, considerable improvement above the 6th grade occurred although none developed reading skills greater than 8th grade.

If the applicant chose not to join the program, he was assigned to a job without prejudice. That is to say, he was routed to those sections where there was no upgrade effort: general helper, warehouseman, etc.

The wage differential, described in Chapter 4, between program and non-program new employees, was offered as an inducement. In three to four weeks, a program entrant could earn more by participating in the program.

Recruitment of Senior Employees

Before taking participants into the program, the union committee met to review the entrance requirements. They thereafter approved the procedures employed. A circular was prepared describing the program and the eligibility requirements. This, together with a form which was to be completed by anyone who was interested, was placed in employee pay envelopes. The circular produced almost a zero response. Upon inquiry, it was discovered that many of the men could not read well, and hence the decision was made to talk to each man personally.

A repeated and extensive effort was made to get senior employees to participate. The same restrictions as applied to new employees was mandatory for senior employees, i.e., disqualification for color blindness and functional illiteracy.

Program Choices

The program was structured to offer both senior and new employees an opportunity to participate in the upgrade program in the print and laminating-embossing departments. New employees could participate in any one of the following:
1. He could take GED education only *(GED Only)*.
2. He could take GED and skill training *(Mixed)*.
3. He could take skill training only *(STO)*.

If skill training was elected, all new employees first entered step one, cutter-backtender training, then, upon successful completion, went on to step two: (a) printer training, or (b) laminator-embossing operator training.

Senior employees were given the same choices, except they bypassed cutter-backtender training if they had worked as a cutter or backtender at Alpha. These routes are shown diagrammatically in Figure 4.1.

Release Time

For those participating in the program, Alpha provided release time for off-site instruction. The employee was paid his regular wage rate for eight hours and was released from work to attend 2 four-hour instructional sessions. (Excluding travel and clean-up time, this actually left slightly more than six hours of time for instruction each week.)

Release time was equally available for new and senior employees. Men used their own cars or the company station wagon to travel to the Training Center which was eight minutes away by auto.

Skill Training and Education

The first phase of the skill training involved learning the *redesigned* cutter-backtender job at the off-site Training Center. This vestibule training took place over a period of three weeks (18 instructional hours). There, the trainees were introduced to the cutter-backtender's job, using a manual which had been prepared for their use. Supported by other collateral materials -- simplified instructional sheets, AV materials, and physical demonstrations -- the trainee was instructed in the terminology of the process, its basic history, and the type of goods he would be expected to work. Basic safety information and machine operation were reviewed. As well, he learned those skills that were part of the redesigned job as a prerequisite to becoming a print trainee.

The time spent on the job (32 hours a week) was supported by an OJT trainer (see below). The man continued to work as a cutter-backtender or, in some instances, was assigned to cover other aspects of production as needed by the company.

Phase two of skill training was directed toward advanced printing or laminating-embossing training. Manuals were used to cover this advanced phase of the program. Basic instruction in print and/or lamination theory and in the principles and control of the machines was carried on at the Training Center. This latter phase of the instruction took approximately 23 additional weeks for the first cycle of print trainees, 17 weeks for the second cycle of trainees. Only one cycle of lamination operator training was given over a period of 6 weeks. (See Table 5.1 for curriculum.)

OJT

In contrast to the less formal instructional methods used by Alpha in the past, the training offered by the contractor was more formal. All materials covered in vestibule training were also demonstrated on the job. The order and intent of job training design was linked to the OJT instruction provided by the trainers on the floor. The OJT trainer directly addressed the problems the trainee was experiencing (such information usually given him by the printer or operator), then worked with the trainee, providing additional instruction to help clear the problem. In addition, the OJT trainer helped the trainee "break the ice" with the crew chief (operator or printer). If there were any "hitches," such as scheduling problems, the OJT trainer was required to solve them.

Trainer Training

The three OJT trainers were selected by management and were Alpha employees. One of the trainers had been a key union officer a year or so before. The trainers were interviewed by the contractor to ascertain their skills as well as their ability to relate to the training population. All three were qualified and accepted. These men were potentially the core trainers for sustaining the formal upgrade effort after the contractor finished his field work and left.

Of the trainers suggested by management, two were assigned to training in the print department and one in laminating-embossing.

The contractor subsequently provided pre-service trainer training for all three over a two-week period on a one-half day basis on release time.

The lesson plans were utilized as a primary focus for the training. The inter-relatedness of OJT training (conducted on the factory floor) and the classroom training was stressed. The trainer learned to provide instructions as they were designated in the manual. In addition, he was provided with a pre-service course in "human relations." This focused primarily on helping the trainer gain insight into the problems participants might have in learning the new job.

Education

Education, together with skills training or education only *(GED Only)*, was given at the off-site Training Center. Supplementary tutoring and individual instruction were provided where necessary. The program was predicated on 160 hours of classroom instruction, which at a rate of 6 hours per week would take approximately 26 weeks for the *GED Only* group. Combined with skills training, the instructional time would ordinarily have taken 52 weeks, except for the fact that it was possible to concentrate large blocks of GED instructional time before *Mixed* skill training cycles started up and after it was completed. Nevertheless, it did take longer than *GED Only*, 34 weeks compared to 26 weeks.

The decision to include education was based on the need to provide basic educational support for trainees entering advanced skill training. The education basically required was limited to reading comprehension so as to increase their ability to use the manuals and instructional sheets and acquisition of the mathematical skills so as to permit computation of such factors as: press running speed, yards-per-minute, total yardage and proportions in ink mixing. It was also predicated on the desire to offer senior employees an opportunity to upgrade their educational skills. As well, employees who had not completed high school could get their equivalency diploma. All employees were at least offered an opportunity to upgrade their reading and math skills, even if they were not interested in getting an equivalency diploma.

In offering *GED Only* or in conjunction with skills training an employee could self-select what he felt was needed to help in getting into an upgrade position.

Instruction was individualized in the context of the program: class size was kept at 10 or fewer students. The class met at the Training Center twice a week, either for six hours of *GED Only;* or for three hours, if taken in conjunction with skills training.

The program consisted of materials which were intended to assist trainees in acquiring basic educational skills or for getting a high school equivalency diploma. The elements included: (a) social science, (b) natural science, (c) literary materials, (d) English usage, and (e) mathematics. In support of these subjects, 74 lesson units were offered, each approximately two hours in length.

The education program was part of a sub-experiment examining the relevance of GED education in employee mobility. A complete description of the GED program is provided in Appendix C.

Progression Steps

Not all employees were expected to complete the full program. An employee-trainee leaving the program could return to work without penalty, e.g., without wage or change of shift penalty. Upon completion of cutter-backtender training, the employee could "get off the ladder" or become a print trainee.[2]

As noted, print training took 23 additional weeks after completion of cutter-backtender. From day-one on the job, the employee-trainee was moved from cutter-backtender through print training over a maximum of 26 weeks. Included in this were delays in cycling (related to scheduling), build up of class size, and so on. The second cycle of print trainees took four months rather than six.

The print trainee or the operator (in laminating-embossing) was assigned to a crew as the fourth member of a three-member crew. This made it possible for the trainer and the printer (or lead operator) to provide additional instructions to the trainee without seriously affecting production on the machine.

---

[2] The same was subsequently true for laminating-embossing training.

To demonstrate his skills, the print trainee was scheduled for a two-week solo period in which he alone ran the press and supervised the crew. In laminating-embossing, this two-week trial was unnecessary. His *graduation* was predicated on his performance rating, a composite of how the trainer and supervisor scored his progress.

Supportive Services

Supportive services were available on an *as needed* basis. At the intake interview and periodically thereafter, program participants were told or reminded of the availability of these services. They were solicited individually for any problem they cared to identify. They could avail themselves of these services as they saw fit, at any time.

Basically, these services consisted of: (a) legal assistance, criminal or civil problems; (b) referral to community-based agencies, hospitals or other services; (c) intervention as an employee-employer referee; (d) counseling; and (e) fiscal assistance, e.g., paying the GED examination fee.

All *problems* were assumed to be job related to the degree that they could potentially interfere with the trainee's ability to perform to the standard of the senior employee. By and large, the support helped trainees to deal with problems that might otherwise have led to behavior that was unacceptable. As such, a weekly meeting was held with the OJT and the vestibule trainer to review all potential and existent problems, including those which were identified in the support offered by other service inputs. These sessions, though primarily focused on training problems, were directed to the trainee's personal problems, either in anticipation of a problem or one that was already existent. Since problems of confidentiality were involved, the results of these meetings (and their recommendations) were only followed up directly. The OJT trainer was solicited for his opinion, but did not deliver any service input. The actual service was delivered by the contractor's staff counselor.

Supportive services was part of a sub-experiment, described in greater detail in Appendix B.

Employer Commitment

Alpha was committed to promoting all successful trainees even if the original manpower projections were exceeded. Although the trainee received the grade and wage, he was not consistently used to fill a printer or operator position. (Alpha was made aware that the alternate assignments would have to include printing or operation of the laminator-embosser. Failure to assign the graduate to a position in which he could continue to practice these new skills would potentially result in a loss of these skills over time. As well, severe morale problems would result.)

Wage scales established for all interim program steps were developed by the company in consultation with the contractor as part of the employer's commitment.

Summary

The upgrade model did not affect the company's usual method of recruiting and hiring employees. Once employed, a variety of program choices were made available to new employees, the same choices as were made available to senior employees. These included: *GED Only*, *Mixed* or *STO*. The latter two, skills training (with GED) and skills training only, lead to printer or lamination operator positions. Supportive services were available on an *as needed* basis to all employees.

The employer was committed to promoting all successful employee-trainees.

Table 5.1
CURRICULUM OUTLINE

CUTTER-BACKTENDER

Cutter

Lesson I	Orientation
Lesson II	Brief history of printing and background information concerning Alpha
Lesson III	Explain all safety precautions to be followed, functions of cutter and operation of delivery unit

Backtender

Lesson IV	Learn proper method of loading and splicing film
Lesson V	Show differences in coloring and various processings of film

Common Job

Lesson VI	Show enrollees construction, characteristics, and names of parts of rotogravure press
Lesson VII	Review press operation and show inking unit, including: construction, characteristics, and operation
Lesson VIII	Show enrollees proper method of exchanging tape and press wash-up
Lesson IX	Show doctor blade mechanism: construction, characteristics, and operation. Also show how to set
Lesson X	Plug-in lesson on exchange of coppers
Lesson XI	Introduction to feeding unit and explanation of backtender's duties

PRINT TRAINEE

Lesson I	Orientation
Lesson II	Introduction to printing process
Lesson III	Introduce enrollees to rotogravure method of printing
Lesson IV	Familiarize trainees with rotogravure process (advanced)
Lesson V	Show enrollees construction, characteristics, and names of parts of rotogravure press
Lesson VI	Review press operation and show inking unit, both construction and operation

Table 5.1 (Cont)

CURRICULUM OUTLINE

Lesson VII	Review materials (check on effectiveness of presentation)
Lesson VIII	Familiarize enrollees with content and meaning of dye-order and get them to think as printers
Lesson IX	Have enrollees "use" typical dye order
Lesson X	Provide some indication of how observer "sees" enrollee when working
Lesson XI	Familiarize enrollees with all steps and procedures to be undertaken in order to operate press. Present information on exchange of coppers. Review OJT training
Lesson XII	Show enrollees exact procedure for correct alignment of cylinders
Lesson XIII	Demonstrate construction, characteristics, and operation of doctor blade, including correct setting. Also demonstrate correct method of cleaning and preparing blade for different wipes
Lesson XIV	Familiarize the enrollees with the content, meaning, and purpose of the Print Production Card. Instruct enrollees as to proper method of completing form
Lesson XV	Familiarize enrollees with purpose of and correct procedure for color matching
Lesson XVI	Present company consultant on mixing of inks
Lesson XVII	Review retention of material by enrollees and the effectiveness of presentations
Lesson XVIII	Familiarize the enrollees with names and characteristics of the most common inks and solvents. In addition, discuss common printing problems and their solution

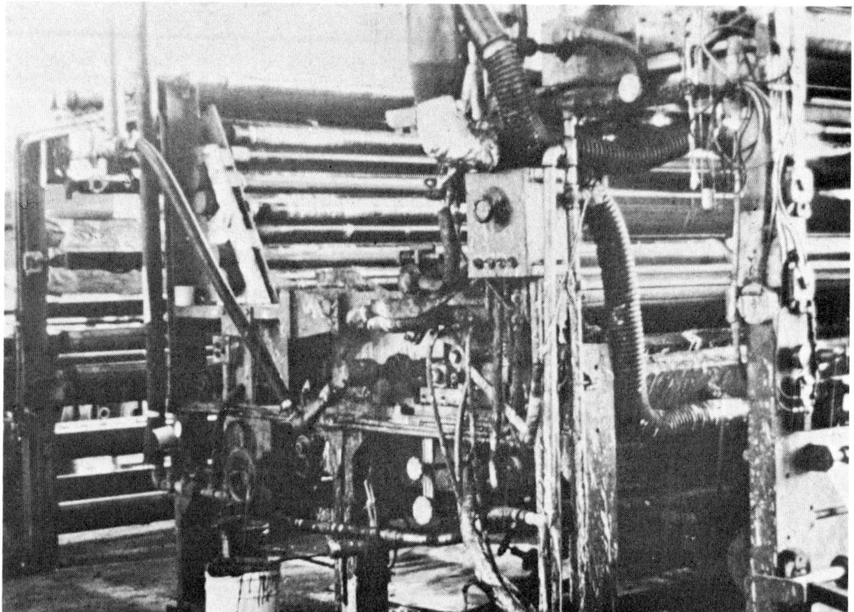

6
Program Particpants

At the outset of the project, a standardized interview procedure was established for all Alpha applicants, whether or not they were hired by the company; the interview was also given all senior employees. The interview was conducted by a member of the contractor's staff. This interview did not supersede Alpha's regular processing procedure. The interview given by the contractor sought to (a) measure program appeal, (b) measure possible creaming of applicants, and (c) provide a more comprehensive empirical description of new employees brought into the company.[1] These data also serve to identify which of the employees would most or least benefit by the upgrading effort.

---

[1] The responses to the questionnaire were not independently confirmed, e.g., by calling the previous employer to ascertain salary, and reason for leaving. The report is based on what the interviewer was told.

New Hires

Two groups of Alpha applicants are contrasted: first, all applicants hired and entering the upgrade program (N=61);[2] second, all new applicants, including those whose applications for employment were rejected, and those hired but not entering the upgrade program (N=53). A composite of these two groups provides a picture of the type of applicant appearing at Alpha's door in the first six months of 1970.

The essential data covering the 61 new hires who became program participants are presented in this chapter. Where there are apparent dissimilarities between the program group and those not hired or entering the program (non-program), a footnote reference has been utilized to detail the differences.

The new employees were all male. The ethnic composition was predominately Black (85%), having a large age spread. Whites were generally young, usually students looking for temporary work (see Table 6.1).

As with other manufacturers utilizing low-wage paying employees, new hires were: (a) older workers who had not been able to find and/or hold higher paying jobs (43%), (b) young, relatively inexperienced workers who had been in the labor force for only a short time (38%), and (c) young workers entering the labor force for the first time, either recently out of school or military service (20%). (See Table 6.2.) Consequently, the average age of the group as a whole was young; 21 years of age. The older, experienced worker, ranging in age from 25 to over 40 years, comprised approximately one-third of the program entrants (see Table 6.3).

Excluding those entering the labor force for the first time, the average time spent in the labor force was five years. During that time, the group as a whole held an average of three full-time jobs with varying periods of unemployment (see Tables 6.4 and 6.5).[3]

---

2 Fifty-eight entered skills training, three entered GED only.

3 While on the average no differences in number of previous jobs were observed between groups, applicants who did not enter the program consisted of a higher percentage of men who had only one job, and a lower percentage of men with five or more jobs. These data indicate some selectivity on the part of the company in excluding younger inexperienced applicants.

While the younger men were single (60%) or married with one child or none (approximately 9%), the older program employees had families with one to five children (32%). (See Table 6.6.)

At the time they applied at Alpha for work, the employment status of applicants indicated that 20% had not previously held full-time jobs because of school or military service. The rest (80%) had been working in a variety of full-time jobs (see Table 6.7). Of the total group, 33% were then working and 48% were unemployed. Their periods of unemployment ranged from one week to over three months; on the average, they were out of work for two months.

Their experience in the labor market was varied, but almost invariably it was in low skilled jobs. Many were helpers; they did the rough work of a material handler, junkyard man or laborer. The relatively skilled men, few in number, had worked boning meat, refinishing air conditioners, working in construction or as mechanic's helpers (see Table 6.8). Weekly earnings, for the group as a whole before deductions, averaged $101. In part, these low wages were related to the low skills requirements of the jobs; in part, to the lower earning ability of the younger workers.

In their previous employment most of the jobs could readily be learned because of their low skills requirement.[4] Most already knew how to do the job when they first started (53%); either that or they picked the skill up by themselves; some were briefly shown how to do it (18%). Some training was required in only one-third of the jobs. These men had held these jobs for varying periods of time. Twenty-eight percent had stayed under three months; 32% up to six months; and 40% longer than six months (see Table 6.10).[5]

Either there was no union at the previous job (57%) or the men did not choose to join (15%). In one-fourth of the jobs, the men joined the union. Even when the interviewer inquired about the presence of a union on the next to last job held, the same findings were reported (see Table 6.11).[6]

---

[4] There was a tendency for men not entering the program to have had jobs not requiring instruction or training. These data are shown in Table 6.9.

[5] Men who had worked at the previous job for short periods of time (under three weeks) and for long periods of time (one year or more) tended not to enter the program.

[6] Among men who entered the program there was a significantly higher number of men who had worked at non-union jobs.

These data suggest that the men drawn to Alpha and the upgrade program come from both the primary and secondary labor markets.

Offsetting the lower wages was the employee's view that the working conditions were satisfactory on his prior job. For example, in describing the work conditions, more than half rated them as good or excellent (56%); the conditions were "O.K." for 13%; and 31% thought them fair to poor (see Table 6.12).[7] Few reported difficulty on the job. When asked whether they had any trouble with anyone, including supervisors and co-workers, 85% answered no; 15%, yes. It is to be remembered that applicants appearing for jobs do not as a rule identify themselves as being unable to get along in previous employment situations.

The loss of the prior job is reported to have occurred for many reasons (see Tables 6.13 and 6.14). In order of most frequent reply, the five main reasons for leaving the job were reported as follows:[8]

Laid-off	32%
Quit to get better job	23%
Quit, didn't like job	15%
Moved	11%
Fired	6%

Whether release from the job was involuntary or self-initiated, most men found it difficult to get another job. Some were out of work for two months before obtaining work at Alpha. (They would have received unemployment insurance over this period.) Most came to Alpha because they needed a job. The existence of a training program, they said, was of less importance than the job itself. Training was important only if it led to more money (see Table 6.15).

Most located their job at Alpha through friends, probably because most of the Alpha workers lived in the local Black community (34%).

[7] Among those not entering the program there was a higher proportion of men rating their previous job as excellent or good (66%) compared to 56% among program entrants.

[8] Non-program applicants more often reported, as the four main reasons for leaving their previous job: quitting to get a better job, 34%; laid-off, 21%; entering military service, 16%; moving, 8%; and sickness or accident, 5%.

Others saw the hiring sign while canvassing for a job (30%); and some, the ads in the local press (15%).

Alpha also notified the local poverty agency and State Employment Service on several occasions that they were hiring workers at a starting wage of $84-90, had a training and upgrading program and were requesting referrals. Only 8% were made up of referrals from the local poverty agency and the State Employment Service. Of the eight men that appeared, two were hired and two rejected the job; four were turned away. Of the latter, three had problems with alcohol and one was handicapped.

Finally, 13% were returning to Alpha as employees who had once left (see Table 6.16).

*

In general, the employment and work status profiles of program entrants and those not entering the program were similar. Some differences emerge in comparing the respective group's prior job experience. These data suggest that those not entering employment or the program at Alpha were more often union members at their previous job, found the working conditions better at their previous job, or had more limited work experience (one job). In addition, the job was easier to learn (less training needed).

The men taking jobs at Alpha had been more frequently laid off. In contrast, men not taking jobs were looking for better jobs than they had.

For those entering the program, a detailed description of their academic status and ability was available. Few had completed high school (18%). Reading achievement scores averaged only 7.7 grade level on the Stanford Achievement Test, paragraph meaning (a measure of reading comprehension). Measured on this basis, 41% were able to read, 31% read with difficulty and 28% were functionally illiterate (scores less than 6th grade). (See Table 6.17.)

In mathematical ability (see Table 6.18), self-ratings were low. Only 34% indicated they had no difficulty in mathematics. When specifically asked about mathematical skills, most said they could add, subtract, multiply and divide. More advanced mathematics such as fractions, percentages, algebra and geometry were less well-known (see Table 6.19).

Senior Employees

Only a few senior employees joined the skills upgrading program (N=8).[9] The small number of such men within this group obviates developing a statistical profile -- as was possible with the applicant group.

Without exception, senior employees were older, white, had been with Alpha for a minimum of one year to a maximum of eight. These were employees who had not been able to advance to the highest skill jobs in the production area. Alpha encouraged these men to participate in the program (although there were others so encouraged who declined to participate); most joined the program to receive more training so as to be eligible for upgrading within their respective production areas.

The reasons why more senior employees did not participate is discussed elsewhere in this study (see Chapter 10).

Summary

Employees who accepted jobs at Alpha and joined the upgrade program fell into three groups:

1. Older workers who had not been able to find and/or hold onto higher paying jobs;
2. Younger workers in the labor force for a short period of time; and
3. Workers entering the labor force for the first time.

These workers were predominately Black. They had been in low-skill, low wage-paying jobs and had experienced two months of unemployment prior to finding a job at Alpha. When compared to other applicants, the reasons given for accepting a job at Alpha were found to be related to their reasons for leaving their previous job (laid-off), type of previous job (low-skill, non-union, poorer working conditions), and their immediate need for a job (money).

Few finished high school. They were poor in mathematical skills and one-third were found to be functionally illiterate.

---

[9] Senior employees also joined the educational program. They are described in Appendix C.

Table 6.1
ETHNIC STATUS

	Program N	Program %	Non-Program N	Non-Program %	Total N	Total %
Black	52	85	41	77	93	82
White	9	15	12	23	21	18
Puerto Rican	(3)		(6)		(9)	
Pakestanian	(1)		(-)		(1)	
Other White	(5)		(6)		(11)	
Total	61	(100)	53	(100)	114	(100)

Table 6.2
EXPERIENCE IN LABOR FORCE

	Program N	Program %	Non-Program N	Non-Program %	Total N	Total %
First time labor force	12	20	9	17	21	18
Inexperienced, few jobs (1-3)	23	38	25	47	48	42
Experienced, many jobs (4-9)	26	43	19	36	45	40
Total	61	(101)	53	(100)	114	(100)

Table 6.3

AGE OF APPLICANTS

	Program N	Program %	Non-Program N	Non-Program %	Total N	Total %
-18	0	--	1	2	1	1
18-21	30	54	28	56	52	49
22-29	18	32	14	28	37	35
33-39	7	13	6	12	13	12
40+	1	2	1	2	3	3
Sub-total (%)	56	(101)	50	(100)	106	(100)
No information	5	--	3	--	8	--
Total	61		53		114	

Table 6.4

TIME IN LABOR FORCE

	Program N	Program %	Non-Program N	Non-Program %	Total N	Total %
Out of labor force	12	20	9	17	21	18
Time in labor force	49	80	44	83	93	82
1 yr.	9	(15)	7	(13)	16	(14)
4 yrs.	21	(34)	19	(36)	40	(35)
9 yrs.	11	(18)	8	(15)	19	(17)
14 yrs.	5	(8)	4	(8)	9	(8)
19 yrs.	1	(2)	2	(4)	3	(3)
20 yrs. +	2	(3)	4	(8)	6	(5)
Total	61	(100)	53	(100)	114	(100)

Table 6.5
NUMBER PREVIOUS JOBS

	Program N	Program %	Non-Program N	Non-Program %	Total N	Total %
1 job	3	6	8	18	11	12
2 jobs	11	22	8	18	19	20
3-4 jobs	18	37	17	39	35	38
5-9 jobs	17	35	11	25	28	30
Sub-total (%)	49	(100)	44	(100)	93	(100)
No information	--	--	--	--	--	--
Out of labor force	12	--	9	--	21	--
Total	61		53		114	

Table 6.6
MARITAL STATUS

	Program N	Program %	Non-Program N	Non-Program %	Total N	Total %
Single	34	60	36	69	70	64
Married/Div/Sep.		40		31		36
0 children	5	(9)	3	(6)	8	(7)
1 child	4	(7)	4	(8)	8	(7)
2 children	5	(9)	2	(4)	7	(6)
3+ children	9	(16)	7	(13)	16	(15)
Sub-total	57	(100)	52	(100)	109	(100)
No information	4		1		5	
Total	61		53		114	

Table 6.7

PRE-ALPHA EMPLOYMENT STATUS

	Program N	Program %	Non-Program N	Non-Program %	Total N	Total %
Out of labor force	12	20	9	17	21	18
Employed	20	33	19	36	39	34
Unemployed		48		47		47
3 weeks	8	(13)	6	(11)	14	(12)
1 month	4	(7)	6	(11)	10	(9)
2 months	7	(11)	6	(11)	13	(11)
3+ months	10	(16)	7	(13)	17	(15)
Total	61	(101)	53	(100)	114	(99)

Table 6.8
LAST JOB HELD, SALARY AND TENURE

Trainee Number	Last Job Held	Weekly Salary ($)	Tenure Last Job
1	Truck driver	75	4 mo.
2	Bagging man	100	5 mo.
3	Helper	100	6 mo.
4	Farm worker	50	10 yrs.
13	Helper, butcher shop	64	1 mo.
16	Dishwasher	80	1 wk.
26	Truck driver	130	7 mo.
28	AC refinishing	145	5 yrs.
33	Junkyard laborer	97	4 mo.
36	Maintenance	90	5 mo.
37	Shipping	95	3 mo.
40	Salesman, hardware	90	1 wk.
42	Material handler	80	5 mo.
49	Maintenance	65	4 mo.
51	Lift truck operator	86	2 mo.
55	Helper, candy wrap	95	6 mo.
56	Truck driver	120	3 mo.
59	Helper	108	1½ yrs.
60	Fork lift operator	150	6 mo.
64	Painter	76	2½ mo.
66	Maintenance	130	1 yr.
67	Junkyard laborer	92	4 mo.
68	Boner, meat market	138	3 yrs.
70	Material handling	98	2 mo.
71	Meat handler	104	7 mo.
72	Gas station attendant	100	7 mo.
79	Cleaning plant, helper	80	6 mo.
82	Repair music instruments	Self-employed	6 mo.
83	Machine operator	54	3 yrs.
87	Taxi driver	125	5 mo.

Table 6.8 (Cont)
LAST JOB HELD, SALARY AND TENURE

Trainee Number	Last Job Held	Weekly Salary ($)	Tenure Last Job
88	General helper	134	7 mo.
90	Mechanic's helper	140	6 mo.
92	Porter	85	3 mo.
93	General laborer	110	9 mo.
94	Machine operator	84	1½ yrs.
95	Mixer, bakery	110	3 mo.
96	In school		
97	Material handler	120	5 mo.
98	Handy man	80	1 yr.
110	Assembly line	100	3 wks.
112	In school		
115	Label containers	128	6 mo.
116	Helper	84	1 mo.
117	In school		
119	Farm worker	125	10 yrs.
121	Salesman, cookware	173	3 yrs.
122	Material handler	80	3 mo.
123	Shipping clerk	60	1 yr.
124	In school		
125	Machine operator	104	1 yr.
126	Laborer	88	1 mo.
127	Military service		
128	Construction	236	1 mo.
129	Install car tape decks	90	1 yr.
131	Janitor	40	9 mo.
132	No information		
133	Military service		
134	No information		
135	No information		
136	Maintenance	65	4 yrs.
137	Packing	94	1 yr.

Table 6.9
JOB DIFFICULTY AT PREVIOUS JOB

	Program N	Program %	Non-Program N	Non-Program %	Total N	Total %
Knew how to do it	24	53	21	49	45	51
Picked it up right away	1	2	7	16	8	9
Showed me how briefly	7	16	6	14	13	15
Needed training	13	29	9	21	22	25
Sub-total (%)	45	(100)	43	(100)	88	(99)
No information	4	--	1	--	5	--
Out of labor force	12	--	9	--	21	--
Total	61		53		114	

Table 6.10
TENURE AT PREVIOUS JOB

	Program N	Program %	Non-Program N	Non-Program %	Total N	Total %
1 month or less	6	13	7	16	13	14
3 months	7	15	8	18	15	16
6 months	15	32	8	18	23	25
1 year	10	21	8	18	18	20
1+ years	9	19	13	30	22	24
Sub-total (%)	47	(100)	44	(100)	91	(100)
No information	2	--	--	--	2	--
Out of labor force	12	--	9	--	21	--
Total	61		53		114	

Table 6.11
UNION PRESENCE

I. Presence of Union at Previous Job

	Program N	Program %	Non-Program N	Non-Program %	Total N	Total %
No union	26	57	15	35	41	46
Yes, but didn't join	7	15	11	26	18	20
Joined union	13	28	17	40	30	34
Sub-total (%)	46	(100)	43	(101)	89	(100)
No information	3	--	1	--	4	--
Out of labor force	12	--	9	--	21	--
Total	61		53		114	

II. Presence of Union, Next to Last Job

	Program N	Program %	Non-Program N	Non-Program %	Total N	Total %
No union	24	59	12	38	36	49
Yes, didn't join	5	12	3	9	8	11
Joined union	12	29	17	53	29	40
Sub-total (%)	41	(100)	32	(100)	73	(100)
No information	8	--	12	--	20	--
Out of labor force	12	--	9	--	21	--
Total	61		53		114	

Table 6.12

RATING: WORKING CONDITIONS PRIOR JOB

	Program N	Program %	Non-Program N	Non-Program %	Total N	Total %
Excellent	4	8	2	5	6	7
Good	23	48	27	61	50	54
O.K.	6	13	3	7	9	10
Fair	11	23	9	21	20	22
Poor	4	8	3	7	7	8
Sub-total (%)	48	(99)	44	(101)	92	(101)
No information	1	--			1	--
Out of labor force	12	--	9	--	21	--
Total	61		53		114	

Table 6.13

TROUBLE WITH SUPERVISOR OR CO-WORKERS AT PREVIOUS JOB

	Program N	Program %	Non-Program N	Non-Program %	Total N	Total %
No	40	85	35	81	75	83
Yes	7	15	8	19	15	17
Sub-total (%)	47	(100)	43	(100)	90	(100)
No answer	2	--	1	--	3	--
Out of labor force	12	--	9	--	21	--
Total	61		53		114	

Table 6.14
REASONS FOR LEAVING PREVIOUS JOB

	Program N	Program %	Non-Program N	Non-Program %	Total N	Total %
Fired	3	6	1	3	4	5
Laid off		32	8	21	23	27
Quit:						
to get better job	11	23	13	34	24	28
didn't like job	7	15	2	5	9	11
before got fired	--	--	1	3	1	1
salary too low	2	4	2	5	4	5
Moved and left job	5	11	3	8	8	9
Sickness/accident	2	4	2	5	4	5
Military service	2	4	6	16	8	9
Sub-total (%)	47	(99)	38	(100)	85	(100)
No information	2	--	6	--	8	--
Out of labor force	12	--	9	--	21	--
Total	61		53		114	

Table 6.15

REASONS FOR WANTING JOB AT ALPHA

Reasons	Program N	Program %	Non-Program N	Non-Program %	Total N	Total %
Need the money	4	7	7	13	11	10
Unemployed, need job	30	49	19	36	49	43
Training program	4	7	6	11	10	9
Seems like nice place	2	3	3	6	5	4
Near home	3	5	2	4	5	4
Like the work	2	3	4	8	6	5
Interested	3	5	1	2	4	4
Friend works here	1	2	2	4	3	3
First job	12	20	9	17	21	18
Total	61	(101)	53	(101)	114	(100)

Table 6.16
HOW APPLICANTS FOUND OUT ABOUT JOB AT ALPHA

	Program N	Program %	Non-Program N	Non-Program %	Total N	Total %
Friends	18	34	16	32	34	33
Newspaper	8	15	8	16	16	16
State Employment Service	2	4	3	6	5	5
Poverty agency	2	4	6	12	8	8
Once worked here	7	13	2	4	9	9
Saw sign, by myself	16	60	15	30	31	30
Sub-total (%)	53	(100)	50	(100)	103	(101)
No information	8	--	3	--	11	--
Total	61		53		114	

Table 6.17
GRADE STATUS/READING ABILITY

	N	%
High School Graduate	11	18
1-2 years High School	14	23
No High School	36	59
Functionally illiterate	(17)	(28)
Reads with difficulty	(19)	(31)
Total	61	100

Table 6.18

SELF-RATING: MATHEMATICAL ABILITY

	N	%
Very well	19	34
Can do, but slowly	27	48
Only simple problems	7	13
Poor, can't do	3	5
Sub-total (%)	56	(100)
No information	5	--
Total	61	

Table 6.19

SELF-RATING: MATHEMATIC OPERATIONS

	Yes N	Yes %	No N	No %	No Inform. N	No Inform. %	Total N	Total %
Can you:								
Add?	56	92	0	0	5	8	61	100
Subtract?	54	89	2	3	5	8	61	100
Multiply?	53	87	3	5	5	8	61	100
Divide?	51	84	5	8	5	8	61	100
Do fractions?	38	62	18	30	5	8	61	100
Do percentages?	36	59	19	31	6	10	61	100
Do algebra?	25	41	31	51	5	8	61	100
Do geometry?	18	30	38	62	5	8	61	100

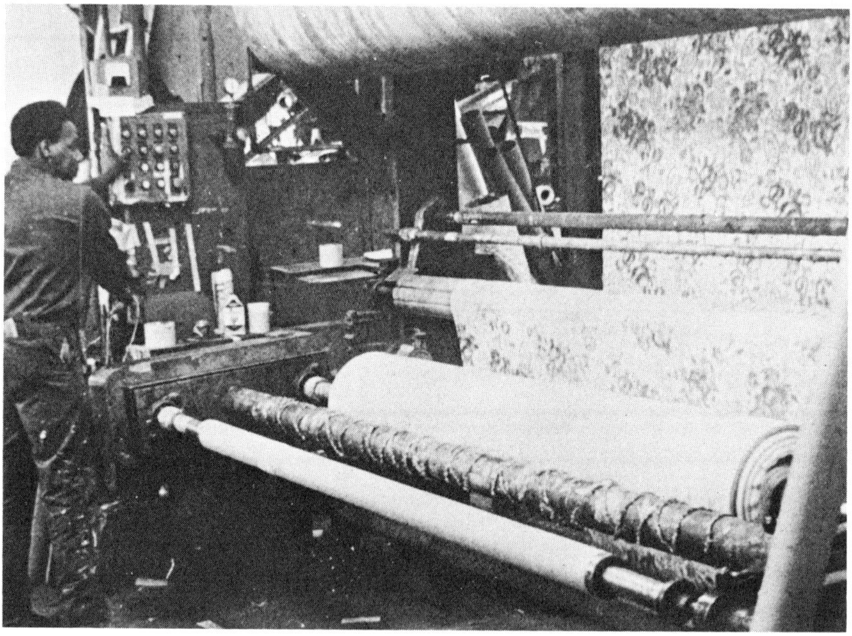

7
Short-term Quantitative Results and Findings

Introduction

The results and findings of the program's impact on employees as of a three-month post-program criteria are reported in quantitative terms in this chapter. The impact of the program in terms of company benefits is reported in Chapter 8. Long-term findings, one year later, are reported in Chapter 9.

Evaluation Issues

The criteria for program upgrade evaluation as applied to employees were as follows:

1. Would the *industry-focused* support of providing Alpha with an upgrade redesign model produce printers in required numbers? (Alpha indicated it could absorb 10 printers.)

2. Would the model work effectively (a) for employee-trainees who were senior employees, and (b) for entry level employees of minority

status (under-educated, under-skilled, and under-employed) who were taken into the program on a "first come, first serve" basis?

3. Would the upgraded employee be able to obtain wage increases commensurate with his increased skills?

4. Would the new hires be constrained from joining the union and thereby not be accorded the same rights, benefits and protection as senior employees?

5. What *employee-supports* were required (education, counseling, and supportive services), and how effective were these services? Would the educational program provide the employee with sufficient skills to pass a high school equivalency examination? Would the education program relate in any cause-effect way to wage/skill upgrading?

6. What was the post-Alpha mobility for employees who left Alpha before or after completing training? Would they get commensurate jobs?

Measurement Criteria

In evaluating the findings, a three-month, short-term status disposition is utilized. The specific program track the employee is following is identified. For example, an employee entering cutter-backtender is first categorized as to whether he did or did not complete the program, and then classified as to whether he remained under three months (left Alpha) or over three months (stayed at Alpha).

If employees went into print training, their disposition is first classified as to whether they did or did not complete print training; and second, as to their tenure at Alpha (under or over three months). However, employees completing print training are evaluated in a longer time frame, since print training took six months.

Wage increases for all employees commensurate with increased skills are reported.

For employees leaving Alpha, a three-month field follow-up was conducted to collect data on: (a) employment disposition, (b) type of job, and (c) salary. These results are compared to the job held at Alpha.

Findings, Industry-Focused Techniques

The data for new hires in skills training is reported first, followed by the data for senior employees entering skills training.

Fifty-eight employees started step one of the printer program which began with training for cutter-backtender (see Table 7.1). Forty-three (74%) completed this step successfully, while 15 (26%) did not complete this step of the program and separated from the program.[1]

Of those 15 not completing step one, 13 left Alpha (22%) and 2 remained at work (3%).

Of those 43 completing step one, 21 (36%) entered step 2, print trainee, while 14 left (24%) and 8 stayed and continued to work at Alpha (14%).

Of the 21 print trainees, 11 (19%) successfully completed the program, while 10 did not. Four of the unsuccessful print trainees left Alpha, while 6 stayed.

As of the three-month status evaluation, 27 of the 58 initial new employees remained at Alpha (47%). From this new employee group, 11 were to be upgraded to printer. (See Table 7.2.)

*

Considering the senior employees only, it is to be noted that 4 who had previously worked as cutter-backtender joined the present program at step two. Three of the 4 successfully completed the training for printer, and 1 terminated employment in a dispute with the General Manager. An additional 4 senior employees entered lamination operator program, and all successfully completed the program.

The fact that 14 employees were becoming eligible for B printer (11 new hires and 3 senior employees) posed a problem for the company. When it became evident that a larger number of new and some senior employees than expected would be completing the printer training after only six months,[2] the company was concerned about its

---

[1] In order to compute program completion rate, when an employee terminated at any program step, he is counted as a loss at that step. Thus, a trainee terminating while training for cutter-backtender is counted as a loss at that point. The loss is expressed as a percent of all others in that same step.

[2] Actual training took 6 months for the first cycle of trainees, and 4 months for the 2nd cycle. The planning period prior to training took 6 months.

Table 7.1

DISPOSITION OF NEW EMPLOYEES ONLY

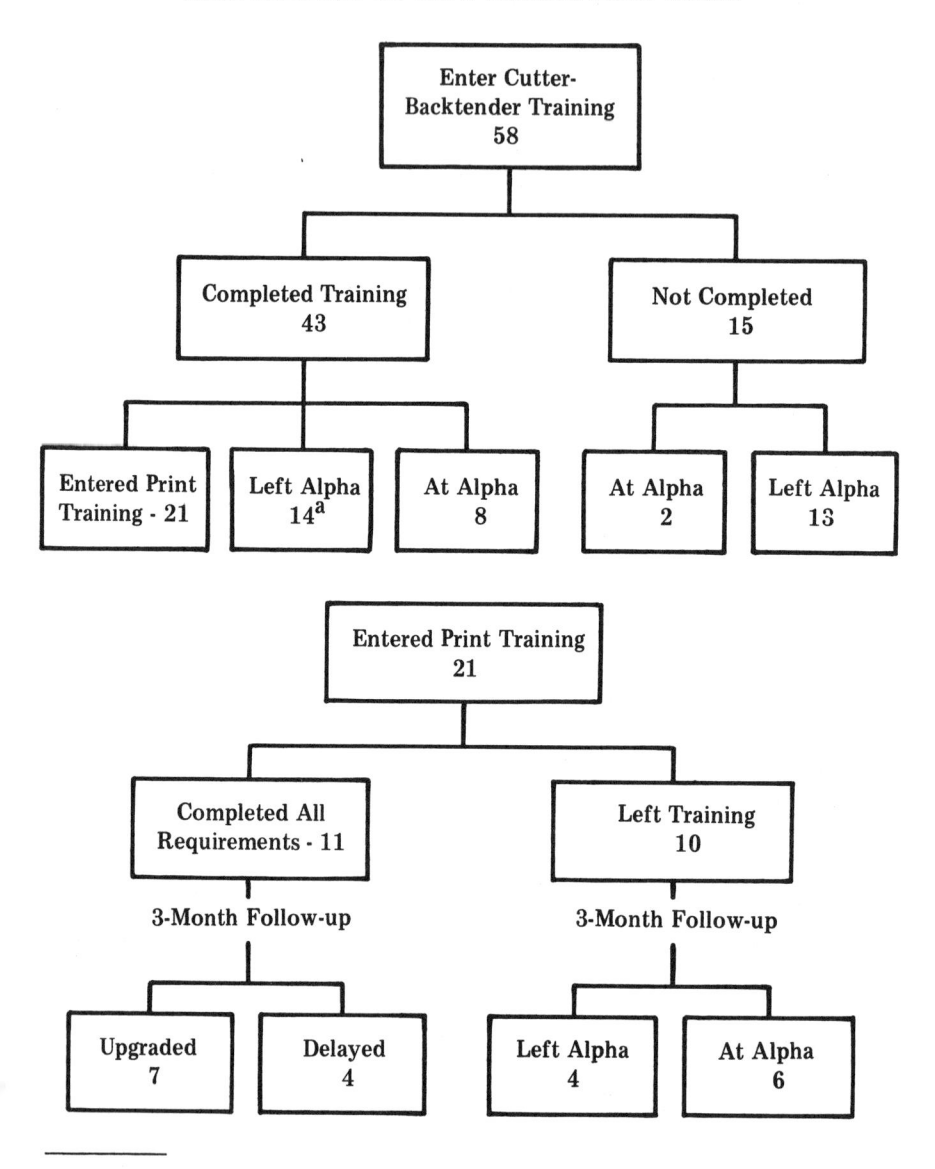

```
                    Enter Cutter-
                  Backtender Training
                          58
                           |
              ┌────────────┴────────────┐
       Completed Training         Not Completed
              43                        15
               |                         |
    ┌──────────┼──────────┐        ┌─────┴─────┐
Entered Print  Left Alpha  At Alpha  At Alpha  Left Alpha
Training - 21    14[a]       8         2          13


                  Entered Print Training
                           21
                            |
              ┌─────────────┴─────────────┐
        Completed All              Left Training
        Requirements - 11                10
    3-Month Follow-up            3-Month Follow-up
              |                            |
        ┌─────┴─────┐                ┌─────┴─────┐
    Upgraded    Delayed          Left Alpha    At Alpha
        7           4                 4            6
```

(a) Of those new employees who completed cutter-backtender training but subsequently left Alpha, 4 entered school, 3 either quit or were fired, 2 went into the Army, 1 went to jail, 1 moved and 3 are unknown regarding their present disposition.

Table 7.2

COMPLETION RATES, ALL TRAINING SEGMENTS[a]
(New Hires Only)

	N	%
ALL ENTER	58	100
COMPLETED CUTTER-BACKTENDER (Step 1)	43	74
Left Alpha	14 (24%)	
Working at Alpha	8 (14%)	
Entered print training	21 (36%)	
Completed print training 11 (19%)		
Terminated training 10 (17%)		
Left Alpha (4)		
Working at Alpha (6)		
DID NOT COMPLETE TRAINING (Step 1)	15	26
Left Alpha	13 (22%)	
Working at Alpha	2 (3%)	

* * * *

3 MONTH FOLLOW-UP		
ALL WORKING AT ALPHA	27	47
ALL LEFT ALPHA	31	53
Subtotal	58	100

(a) Excluding 3 new employees in GED only. Otherwise includes all trainees coming into program. Two new trainees stayed for 1 session, then terminated Alpha. They are counted as program losses.

ability to absorb these employees in printer positions. As well, they were concerned whether the men were in fact adequately trained over such a short period of time.

A program modification was presented by the contractor and accepted by the company to serve as final certification before promotion to B printer. The modification was in the form of an add-on two-week solo trial period for all print trainees to demonstrate their ability to run the presses.

The solo trial period was supervised by the company. The shift foreman, supervisor and OJT trainer served as observers and the production output was checked for quantity and quality. The trainee could seek assistance (as could all printers) but the full responsibility, including crew management, was his. Since only 2 men could be processed through the solo trial period because of production demands, it took about two months before all print trainees were observed and certified.

All 14 print trainees passed their solo trial period; only 1 was judged border-line, but he was passed. Recommendations for promotion to B printer were given to the President of the company by the General Manager, as the men completed their solo trial period.

Finding 1: Redesign Model. The upgrade job redesign model produced printers in sufficient numbers; in fact, it over-produced printers, exceeding the company's absorption ability.

a. A total of 14 employees, 11 new hires and 3 senior employees completed step two, print training, including a two-week solo trial period. The company had expected 10 printers; this exceeded its absorption rate.

b. Because of economic reasons,[3] 7 (including 3 senior employees) were promoted to full-time printer positions; 3 were promoted, but were only to be used as printers in a substitute capacity. They received no increment, but were to receive printer wages when working as printers. Four were promised printer positions at first availability.

Finding 2: Upgrading. The upgrade program served to upgrade both new and senior employees concurrently. New employees were of minority status, had previously worked in low skilled jobs and were under-educated.

a. Because of seniority rules, all senior employees (N=3) were hired into the 7 full-time openings, together with 4 new employees, while some of the new hires were substitutes or awaiting promotion (N=7).

3 See Finding three.

b. New employees completing step one and/or step two, plus those who stayed at Alpha, irrespective of program completion, account for 47% of the new employees. They were absorbed into Alpha's productive system and remained in employment as of the three-month evaluation.

c. The trainee profile data for the group, shown in Table 7.3, point up the characteristics of those who were able to complete the print program. The table shows the individual variations in these data, while the following discussion summarizes the group as a whole.

As a group, successful trainees were not distinguishable from unsuccessful trainees with respect to demographic and employment (work history) variables. Motivational variables were not measured. The data does indicate the reason for the company's surprise at finding that these men could make it -- become qualified printers.

Successful trainees were predominately Black (82%), young (23 years of age), and had been in the labor force for 5 years. Most of the men were single; those who were married averaged 1½ children. Two men had just come out of the army, while the rest worked in unskilled jobs, such as helper, maintenance man, janitor, and hospital linen room attendant. Only 1 man had been in a semi-skilled job working as an air-conditioner refinisher. Most of the men had held their previous jobs an average of 4 months, 2 for an average of 4½ years. They had earned in their previous jobs from $40 a week as a janitor to $145 as an air-conditioner refinisher. The average wage for the group was $92 per week. Before coming to Alpha, they were out of work for approximately 11 weeks.

In reading comprehension, the grade level for the group was 7.0 as compared to 7.7 for the total of the new employee-trainee population.

These data, although small in numbers, tend to profile individuals who would be considered as entry level by the Alpha personnel officer, i.e., as under-educated and low-skilled. Because of irregular work periods (plus low salary), many men were not much above the poverty level; some earned below the poverty level.

Finding 3: Wage Increments. Employees received wage increases commensurate with their increased skills until the final step of the print progression ladder. At that point, the company was resistant to fulfilling their full commitments but the company did meet union scale. In some instances, when the new employee was promoted to printer, the increase from entry level to printer was relatively large

$84 to $120,[4] a 43% increase. While these large increases were given by the company and were union scale, they were below the wage scale initially promised ($140). The company deferred the higher wage payment, expecting that the *new* union contract, to be negotiated 6 months later (July 1971), would give the men approximately a $10 increase. The 3 senior employees completing printer training also earned increases relative to their tenure at Alpha; some were already earning near the maximum union scale. As a consequence, their increment ranged from $10 to $33.

The wage increments varied with respect to the extent of program completion and the company's predilection toward individual trainees. Most employees completing step one, cutter-backtender, but electing *not* to continue on to step two, increased in wages from $84 to $89.

Some men did not want to proceed further; some because they were viewed negatively by supervisors. The company did not feel obligated to increase their wages; they procrastinated, extending the period before increments were paid. Consequently, employees left or were forced out of Alpha. Those electing to continue into step two increased their salary from $84 to $110, a $16 increase.[5]

Upon completing print training and receiving company acknowledgment, 2 new employees received $130 and 2 received $120. The remaining 7, who were substitute printers (promised first call on openings), continued to receive $110; no increment. Wage increases, consequently, ranged from $100 to $130, a $30 increase (30%); $84 to $120, a $36 increase (43%); and $84 to $110, a $26 increase (31%). The wage data for all trainees are shown in Table 7.4.

In addition to the 58 skills trainees, a small group (3) of new hires entered only the education program. One terminated the company having received only a $4 increase; the other 2 remained at work. One employee received no raise; the other, $4. The four dollars was given as a token incentive to stay at Alpha because both were considered good employees.

---

4 In December, 1970 all union members were to get a contractual increase of $.08/hr (excluded from this figure).

5 There were two exceptions, where the employees were already earning $110 because they had been rehired by Alpha at their old job rate after being away for more than a year.

The data indicate that education was not viewed by the company in the same light as skills training, and was less rewarding within this company in monetary terms.

As indicated above, all salaries were expected to increase across the board as a result of contract negotiations six months later. The company sought to use these mandated increases as a substitute for its promise of an increment upon successful completion of the program. Successful trainees had expected two increments, one because of promotion plus an add-on because of the new contract. Wherever it could, the company sought to reduce its wage commitments.

Some trainees discontinuing the program did not get increases; others did but their wages were still low. Some employees, passing all requirements, were not given differential increments.

Employees known to be dissatisfied with the company were passed by. Others received only one increment. Employees earning above average were also passed by. The most vocal, the most active union members, and men the company accepted, received full wage gains.

All employees were angry at not receiving as much money as they thought they should receive; salary increment delays were invariably a cause of contention.

Senior employees who completed lamination operator training were not required to pass a solo trial period. All these men had been at Alpha; consequently, they earned more than the newer employees. Their increments were smaller, ranging from $4 to $10. These data are shown in Table 7.4.

Finding 4: Union Benefits. All employees who stayed at Alpha became members of the union, Local 1200. They were awarded all union rights after 30 days.

The structure of the program required the company to hire employees so that from day one they accumulated time toward union membership. Of the 58 new employees, 15 who left Alpha without completing cutter-backtender did not become union members. All of the remaining 43 new hires became union members.

The status of a union member was better than that of a non-union member. The benefits of union and non-union members are contrasted on the page following.

UNION MEMBERS	NON-MEMBERS
Ten days, holiday	None
Sick leave; coverage on 80% of all medical and drug; 100% hospital to $500+80% coverage	None
Major medical, $10,000	None
Vacation 1 week = 6 months 2 weeks = 1 year 3 weeks = 10 years	None
Can have time for jury duty with pay	None
Three personal days	At discretion of Alpha
$3,000 life insurance	None
Seniority rights	None
Grievance procedures arbitration	None, except as an individual
Double time after 12 hrs. Sunday and holidays; 1½ time Saturdays	At Alpha's discretion

Findings, Employee-Focused Techniques

The details of the programs (and data tables) in employee supports are appended to this study: for supportive services, in Appendix B; for education, in Appendix C. The findings are briefly summarized below.

Finding 5: Employee-Focused Techniques. Employee supports were necessary and could, with some limitations, be supplied within an industrial context. The employee supports were secondary to the basic job redesign model and training mix used in support of the design. Employee supports were needed in education to assist the trainee to understand the manuals and in supportive services for those who were facing problems that would have affected their work and training status.

Education

The GED program was offered in two forms: (a) *GED Only* -- without skill training -- for those interested in trying to obtain a high school equivalency degree; and (b) GED plus skills, in conjunction with skills training *(Mixed).*

Fourteen of 17 new employees (82%) elected GED *Mixed* participation. The opposite trend was followed by senior employees: 10 of 14 (71%) elected *GED Only*. This pattern of program selection relates to the low interest expressed by senior employees toward entering advanced print training. (Only 4 entered advanced print training and 4 entered training for lamination operator.) *Senior employees currently earning relative higher salaries apparently did not want to enter a training program which could not appreciably increase their income. Perhaps the prime incentives for senior employees to enter education was (a) their inability to read (self-image), (b) the company paid for the release-time, and (c) there was no threat of job loss if the program was not successfully completed.*

On the other hand, new employees were less interested in education, and were primarily motivated toward specific job training. In the opinion of new employees, the most important program elements in order of importance were: (a) time to practice and work at the advanced job; (b) skill instruction followed by practice, and (c) education which was useful but "not going to get them the job."

While the training program was viewed as more important than education, even the program format offered in this project -- off-site instruction plus OJT -- was considered less important than a lot of OJT time running the presses. (This attitude was pronounced, notwithstanding the fact that they would not have produced a good product without detailed instruction in print theory.)

The educational levels of employees entering GED were low. Thirty-two percent scored less than 6th grade; 29%, below 7th grade. At best, 61% of all those entering education were marginal readers.[6] The grade level mean for the entire group was 7.6.

As expected, because of firings and terminations, attrition rates for new employees (59%) exceeded those of senior employees (36%). Other reasons for terminations included the length of time to complete the program, the amount of work required and dissatisfaction with their rate of progress or the program itself. The data indicate that educational services must be of shorter duration or the program will begin to suffer from attrition.

For those who stayed with the program, approximate gains of 1 grade per 57 instructional hours were achieved. This rate of progress was related to the initial reading level of the employee. The lower the educational status, the greater the number of hours to get a measurable grade increase. For less than 6th grade, it was 126 hours; less than 7th grade, 50 hours; less than 8th grade, 42 hours.

It is interesting that trainees in *Mixed* gained more than *GED Only*, notwithstanding more time spent in *GED Only*. This is attributed to the greater motivation of new employees. (Senior employees terminated because the education took a long time and was difficult, while new employees left because of difficulty with the company.)

Sufficient instructional hours were not logged by participants due to schedule and work routines; therefore, few passed the equivalency examination.

The program did improve reading and math skills and thereby supported the trainee's ability to read and understand the training manuals.

---

6 Stanford Reading Achievement, paragraph meaning.

Supportive Services

Supportive services was run as a sub-experiment. It was directed toward empirically defining the types of problems identified by employees and testing methods of problem resolution which could prove feasible in an industrial context.

In order to measure the need for these services, employees in the program and supervisors were actively canvassed. The latter group was asked to identify those problems faced by employees in which the contractor's staff could be of some assistance. Where there was an arrest, the need for assistance was overt; where there were other difficulties, it was necessary to define the problem as it directly impacted upon the employee's work proficiency. Absenteeism, lateness, health, distractability related to safety were used as prime indices. The major observations were:

1. A large number of employees, seen repeatly in varying contexts, identified no problems or elected to resolve them by themselves (42% of all trainees).

2. The remaining employees (N=40) identified 75 problems for resolution, indicating a high percentage of multiple problems.

3. Problems were unsatisfactorily resolved in instances of drug use (16% of all problems), alcoholism, homosexuality and apparent psychological disturbances (13% of all problems). In addition, 28% of all problems identified were not resolved either because there was no such service in the community, the agency would not accept the referral, the employee refused to go, or the problem required long-term social services.

4. Some 43% of the problems identified were serviced effectively. These areas included: (a) legal assistance, (b) counseling, (c) special intercession to assist employee with agency, and (d) referral to community agencies.

Operational problems included: (a) the large amount of time required to serve the employee, and (b) the difficulty of anticipating problem areas and developing referral routes to community agencies.[7]

On the favorable side, relatively low costs (excluding staff wages) were incurred in the delivery of services by program staff directly.

---

[7] Published descriptions of services are often non-existent. The agencies are over-crowded and require prolonged application procedures.

These services could have been administered within the personnel department of a company.

There is some indication that supportive services did not markedly reduce turnover at entry level, although it was of utility to a large number of upgraded employees. In effect, it protected the training investment.

The data are interpreted as favorable. All types of supportive services was judged to be feasible within an industrial context. These generally included legal assistance, counseling and referrals to community agencies; in other instances, direct intercession in the work environment was undertaken to work out problems between the employee and his supervisor. The problems which arose are typical of industry; most often, they are "worked out" happenstantially.

Finding, Post-Separation Field Follow-Up

Finding 6: Three-Month Follow-up. Most trainees were able to secure jobs paying higher wages. Many employees who left initially experienced long periods of unemployment, ranging from 3 weeks to 3 months and more. The type of job bears no direct skills relationship to the type of training received at Alpha.

Employees terminating Alpha, whether self- or company-initiated, were followed up 3 months after their separation. The follow-up study covered all employee-trainees separated for three months as of October 1970. The total number who separated at that time was 29. The overall follow-up completion rate was 62% or 18 trainees (see Table 7.5).

The follow-up study centered on the employee's employment status (employed or unemployed). If employed, in what type of job, the salary and whether promotional opportunities were available. For purposes of analysis, company-initiated firings or an employee quitting because of conflict with the company are classified as *unfavorable terminations;* those who self-initiated the job termination because of a desire to return to school, find another job, or enter the armed services are classified as *favorable terminations.* The data are further classified as to how much of the upgrade program employees completed before leaving; i.e., if they *completed* step one, cutterbacktender, or were *incomplete* (did not finish step one). Together with the type of termination, four sub-groups are formed. The data regarding these sub-groups are summarized below.

1. *Incomplete Step One, Unfavorable.* Of the 8 employees falling into this category, 2 were out of the labor force and 2 were unemployed. The 4 that were employed found jobs one to two months later at wages higher than paid by Alpha. All were in low skill jobs, e.g., material handler, stacker in a container plant, and a window washer.

2. *Incomplete Step One, Favorable.* No employees fell into this category.

3. *Completed Step One, Unfavorable.* Of the 4 employees, 1 was arrested and in jail, 1 was unable to secure employment, and the remaining 2 were working (one as a porter).

4. *Completed Step One, Favorable.* Five of the 6 employees were out of the labor force, having returned to school or because of military service. One man had moved.

Summary

The results of a three-month post-program follow-up are reported and found to have produced significant outcomes for both senior and new employees in a program employing (a) industry-focused job redesign upgrade techniques, and (b) employee-focused techniques.

On The Positive Side:

1. More printers than anticipated were produced and qualified for promotion through the utilization of job redesign and promotion ladders.

2. A high rate of program completeness occurred at all skill levels. (For new employees, 20% as printers, 74% as cutter-backtenders; for senior employees, 75% as printers, 100% as operators.)

3. Wage increments commensurate with increased skills (by union standard, but not by company agreement) were obtained by most employees who were already earning higher wages.

4. In education, employees gained one-grade level for every 57 hours of instruction and were able to improve their basic skills.

These gains did not relate (directly or indirectly) to actual upgrading but were secondary benefits.

5. Supportive services was able to satisfactorily resolve 43% of all problems identified and provided needed assistance for upgraded employees. Delivery of supportive services appears to be feasible as part of the services offered within an industrial context.

On The Negative Side:

1. The over-production of printers created absorption problems for the company.

2. Because of the turndown in the economy, the company did not fully meet its commitment to wage increase; it did pay union scale. The employees were resentful of the company's failure to meet its announced commitment, as well as the delays in receiving monies owed. The company did not improve the morale of its employees as a by-product of the upgrade system.

3. In education, most participants failed to pass the high school equivalency examination. This is attributed to the length of the program. It also stemmed from the need to meet production demands This resulted in a circumstance which frequently did not permit the employee to log a sufficient number of hours in educational instruction to complete this phase of the program.

4. Employee-trainees, quitting or fired, upon leaving the company, when followed-up in the field 3 months post-separation, were found to be employed after lengthy periods of unemployment at higher wages but in low skilled jobs with little opportunity for advancement.

Table 7.3

DEMOGRAPHIC CHARACTERISTICS, COMPLETE PRINTER TRAINING

(New Hires Only)

Trainee	Ethnic	Age	Rd. Grade	Mar. Status	No. Children	Out of Work	Previous Job Type of Job	Previous Job Salary	Previous Job Tenure	Time in Labor Force
03	B	21	5.8	M	0	0	Helper	$ 100	6 mo.	2 yrs.
28	B	42	5.8	M	2	3 mo.	AC refin.	145	5 yrs.	15 yrs.
36	B	18	5.6	S	0	10 mo.	Linen Rm.	90	5 mo.	1 yr.
64	B	19	8.6	S	0	2 mo.	Painter	76	2½ mo.	3 yrs.
111	W	22	9.0+	S	0	3 wks.	Helper	84	4 wks.	6 yrs.
115	B	31	6.6	M	3	1 wk.	Labeling	128	6 mo.	12 yrs.
117	B	21	6.8	S	1	1 mo.	Assembly	100	17 days	3 yrs.
127	B	21	5.3	M	0	------	Army	------	------	------
131	W	18	8.4	S	0	0	Janitor	40	9 mo.	2 yrs.
133	B	20	7.6	M	2	------	Army	------	------	------
136	B	19	7.4	S	1	4 mo.	Maint.	65	4 yrs.	4 yrs.
Averages	B-82%	23 yrs.	7.0	S-55% M-45%	1½ Child.	11 wks.		$ 92		5 yrs.

Table 7.4

ALL WAGE CHANGES:
ENTERING, TERMINAL AND CURRENT

I. EDUCATION ONLY

Trainee No.	Initial Wage	Term. Wage	Current Wage	Wage $ Gain
1[a]	$ 82	$ 86		$ 4
70	82		$ 86	4
128	84		84	0

II. CUTTER-BACKTENDER - INCOMPLETE (LEFT)

Trainee No.	Initial Wage	Term. Wage	Current Wage	Wage $ Gain
13	$ 84	$ 84		$ 0
16	82	82		0
40	82	82		0
72	84	84		0
88	84	84		0
92	84	96		12
93	84	96		12
95	84	96		12
96	84	96		12
117	84	84		0
123	84	84		0
129	84	84		0
132	84	84		0

(a) Completed program.

Table 7.4 (Cont'd)

ALL WAGE CHANGES:
ENTERING, TERMINAL AND CURRENT

III. CUTTER-BACKTENDER[b] - INCOMPLETE (STAY)

Trainee No.	Initial Wage	Term. Wage	Current Wage	Wage $ Gain
		Weekly Wage		
55	$ 84		$ 84	$ 0
56	84		84	0

CUTTER-BACKTENTER - COMPLETED (LEFT)

Trainee No.	Initial Wage	Term. Wage	Current Wage	Wage $ Gain
		Weekly Wage		
2	$ 84	$ 84		$ 0[c]
26	84	84		0[d]
33	82	86		4
42	84	84		0[e]
51	82	94		12
66	84	96		12
67	84	100		16
71	84	100		16
79	84	100		16
82	84	88		4
87	84	88		4
94	84	96		12
124	84	84		0[d]
137	84	84		0

(b) Cutter-backtender, no print, with or without GED.
(c) Entered Navy before receiving wage increment.
(d) Did not receive increment.
(e) Did not receive increment, was on probation, left.

Table 7.4 (Cont'd)

ALL WAGE CHANGES:
ENTERING, TERMINAL AND CURRENT

V. CUTTER-BACKTENDER - COMPLETE (STAY)

Trainee No.	Initial Wage	Weekly Wage Term. Wage	Current Wage	Wage $ Gain
4	$ 84		$ 84	$ 0[d]
83	82		96	14
90	84		100	16
98	84		84	0[d]
115	97		103	6[g]
125	84		84	0[d]
126	84		84	0[d]
134	82		86	4

VI. ENTER PRINT - INCOMPLETE[f] (LEFT)

Trainee No.	Initial Wage	Weekly Wage Term. Wage	Current Wage	Wage $ Gain
59	$ 84	$110		$ 26
60	84	110		26
119	84	110		26
121	84	110		26

(f) One Trainee stayed, all others left.

(g) Initial rate high because employee had left Alpha and returned after being away 1+ years.

Table 7.4 (Cont'd)

ALL WAGE CHANGES: ENTERING, TERMINAL AND CURRENT

VII. ENTER PRINT - INCOMPLETE (STAY)

Trainee No.	Initial Wage	Weekly Wage Term. Wage	Current Wage	Wage $ Gain
37	$ 90		$ 94	$ 4[g]
49	110		110	0
68	84		110	26
97	84		110	26
122	84		110	26
123	84		110	26

VIII. ENTER PRINT - COMPLETE (STAY)

Trainee No.	Initial Wage	Weekly Wage Term. Wage	Current Wage	Wage $ Gain
3	$100		$130	$ 30
28	100		130	30
36	84		110	26
64	84		110	26
110	84		110	26
112	84		120	36
116	84		110	26
127	84		110	26
131	84		120	36
133	84		110	26
136	84		110	26

Table 7.4 (Cont'd)
ALL WAGE CHANGES:
ENTERING, TERMINAL AND CURRENT

IX. SENIOR EMPLOYEES - PRINTERS

	Weekly Wage			
Trainee No.	Initial Wage	Term. Wage	Current Wage	Wage $ Gain
44	$ 84	$ 96		$ 12
45	132		$142	10
53	82		97	15
58	100		133	33

X. SENIOR EMPLOYEES - LAMINATION OPERATORS

	Weekly Wage			
Trainee No.	Initial Wage	Term. Wage	Current Wage	Wage $ Gain
17	$ 95		$104	$ 9
81	99		109	10
109	103		113	10
114	131		135	4

Table 7.5

THREE-MONTH FIELD FOLLOW-UP, POST-PROGRAM EMPLOYMENT STATUS
(New Trainees Only)

I. INCOMPLETE STEP 1, CUTTER-BACKTENDER

Unfavorable Termination

Trainee No.	Why Terminated	Period Unempl.	New Job	New Salary ($)	3 Month Empl. Status
13	Fired	5 mo.	Roofer	80	U
40	Quit	3 mo.	none	na	U
72	Quit	3 wks.	Mater. Handler	130	E
88	Quit	1 mo.	Stacker	100	E
92	Quit	2 mo.	Window Washer	120	E
93	Quit	ni	ni	ni	E[a]
123	SDS Active[b,c]	Left to return to college		na	OLF
129	SDS Active[b,c]	Left to return to college		na	OLF

Favorable Termination

None

Note: E = Employed; U = Unemployed; OLF = Out of labor force; na = not applicable; ni = no information.

(a) Relative indicated he was working.

(b) Suspected SDS member seeking factory experience, generally temporary. Plans to return to school.

(c) Stayed 1 session only.

Table 7.5 (Cont'd)
THREE-MONTH FIELD FOLLOW-UP, POST-PROGRAM EMPLOYMENT STATUS
(New Trainees Only)

II. COMPLETE STEP 1, CUTTER-BACKTENDER

Unfavorable Termination

Trainee No.	Why Terminated	Period Unempl.	New Job	New Salary ($)	3 Month Empl. Status
26	Fired	2 mo.	Porter	90	E
51	Fired	ni	ni	ni	E[a]
66	Arrested	na	In jail	na	OLF
79	Quit	4 mo.	none	na	U

Favorable Termination

Trainee No.	Why Terminated	Period Unempl.	New Job	New Salary ($)	3 Month Empl. Status
1[e]	School	na	na	na	OLF
2	Navy	na	na	na	OLF
67	Moved[d]	na	General Factory	95	E
82	School[b]	na	na	na	OLF
87	School[b]	na	na	na	OLF
137	Navy	na	na	na	OLF

Total All Completed	18
Scheduled for follow-up	29
Completion rate (18 of 29)	62%

(d) Moved to California, job waiting

(e) GED only.

8

Economic Effects Of Upgrading For Company

Alpha did not initially have a systematic upgrading mechanism. The company was experiencing problems in retention of its entry level labor force, and in recruitment of workers in the higher skill areas of printer and lamination operator.

Turnover Rates

In the upgrade design tested at Alpha, reducing turnover was prerequisite to obtaining the higher skilled employees. The presence of a systematic upgrade program, it was hypothesized, would reduce turnover, improve productive efficiency and quality of goods.

Turnover was measured by tracking all new employees for six months post-hiring (see Table 8.1). This same method was used to track all program participants as compared to non-program new hires (see Tables 8.2 and 8.3). These data are compared with turnover rates for similar production workers over the same time periods in the previous year (1969). (See Table 8.4.)

In 1970, because of the lower turnover rates of the upgrade participants, overall turnover rates declined approximately 10% compared to 1969. Turnover rates of non-program participants for 1970 were the same as pre-program rates in 1969 (see Table 8.5). However, turnover rates for program entrants declined 19% compared to 1969. At the end of 6 months, 53% of the program entrants had left Alpha, compared to 73% for new hires in 1969.

It may be concluded from these data that turnover rates declined markedly for program participants compared to non-program participants and new employees hired the previous year. It is important to stress that turnover did not drop to insignificant levels (53% left in 6 months), and that the attrition in the trainee sample will continue, but at a much slower rate.

The data support the hypothesis that a systematic upgrade program may enhance employment tenure. Alpha would thus have profit gains to the extent that retention of the entry level labor force reduced wastage costs during training and quality control losses that would otherwise have occurred when new employees were broken in. These profit gains would accrue even though the program participant only finished cutter-backtender training. The job redesign required that the trainee be able to cut yardage from the running web with minimal wastage as the very first skill requirement (see Chapter 4 on job redesign). He was also trained to recognize quality failures while working at his station.

During the training of cutter-backtenders, it was not possible to assign an exact dollar value to possible savings in less wastage and greater quality control, or the costs of breaking in non-program participants. However, the reader should be alert to the fact that turnover losses do not produce excessive company costs in this type of production structure.

The reader should also be alert to selectivity factors that may have contributed to these results. Although all new employees were accepted on a "first come, first serve" basis, only those interested in training and upgrading signed up for the program. These trainees must, therefore, be considered to be *different* from those not interested in the program. As well, there were some instances in which an employee could not immediately enter the program because all on-going training cycles were filled. He, therefore, had to wait for a new cycle. Implicitly, if he waited 2-3 weeks for the next program cycle, he was already manifesting some degree of tenacity in staying with the company.

Production Analysis

Did the upgrade program have any effect in Alpha's productive efficiency? Since the company was losing money because of high skill manpower shortages and poor work quality, it was hypothesized (at the outset) that the upgrade program would have positive impact on Alpha's productivity.

Because of production requirements, it was not possible to hold trainees to specific presses and contrast their productivity to others. They were assigned to different machines at different times and, on finishing the program, they constituted the majority in numbers of production workers on the floor on all shifts. Consequently, production data for all presses is grouped.

In the early months of 1970, only cutter-backtenders had been trained. By September, print trainees were placed on machines; through October, they were completing their solo trial periods. Consequently, time trends are analyzed.

In effect, there is no precise estimate of the exact dollar value, gain or loss, that can be assigned to a specific group of trained printers over others. At best, there are correlations which show that as employee-trainees took over more-and-more of the production Alpha's productive efficiency increased.

During the different months throughout 1969 and 1970, the company received varying print orders. Execution of these orders required different degrees of printing skill, numbers of setups and varied in the ease and length of various production runs. To resolve these variations between months and years for analysis purposes, Alpha's *standard of production* is used.

The standard is individually defined for every type of print order. In any month, the production mix might be expected to vary. However, it is possible to reconcile these variations by reference to the standard. The standard describes, in yardage terms, what should be produced for a specific product-print mix. The concept of *standard* utilized in the table is the *expected* number of yards of all goods printed.

The standard is Alpha's own ongoing criterion for judging productivity. It is reviewed by both management and the union, and accepted as a criteria for incentive payments made in terms of productive achievements (averages). The standard represents the number of yards-per-month produced on the average for each type of goods (in terms of yield, color match, type of material, etc.). This standard was developed over a period of seven years and represents the actual average yardage produced by Alpha in the past on that specific product mix. It has been revised only when there was a change in the printing method. No change in technology occurred in 1969 or 1970. The last change in the standard occurred in early 1968 when it was upgraded 15% because of engineering changes made to the print machines; there was no change in lamination. There have been no changes since. Thus, the base standard for 1969 versus the standard for 1970 is comparable (see Tables 8.6 and 8.7).

The term *actual* utilized in the table indicates the actual number of yards produced in a given month, and the term *difference* indicates the number of yards produced in excess or loss relative to the standard for a given month (shown by sign + or -).

To understand Table 8.6, it should be noted that the production for all four print machines at Alpha was totaled for yards produced, obtained from Alpha's Monthly Production Report. The standard in the monthly report, as noted, is not the same figure for 1969 and 1970, because it reflects variations in the types of goods printed.

For all men employed in production, the standard was important because it was used as the criterion for computing the amount of money earned under the Alpha incentive system, their incentive being computed on the basis of the increase in actual yards over the standard. Thus, in deriving the figures shown, the source utilized was the monthly production figures because of its accuracy as a record of the actual number of yards produced in both the printing and laminating departments, and because there was consensus as regards its use.

The information developed from the monthly report is cumulative for all shifts on all machines at Alpha.

In order to understand the tables, it is also necessary to understand how gains or losses are computed:

1. If there was an increase over standard for both 1969 and 1970, say 10 and 20, respectively, the 1970 gain was +10, a difference over what was accomplished in 1969. If it were 20 and 10 in 1970, the loss would be -10.

2. If both figures show a decline relative to standard, say -10 in 1969 and -20 in 1970, there was a relative loss of -10 in 1970. If the reverse were true, -20 and -10, a relative gain of +10 would show.

3. If 1969 showed a relative gain of +10 and 1970 a loss of -20, the 1970 relative loss would be -30. If the reverse were true, then a +30 would show for 1970.

The *actual* monthly gains or losses for 1970 are shown in the tables as well as the *cumulative* gains or losses for 1970.

Productivity Outcomes in Printing

Table 8.6 summarizes the production data for print yardage produced in 1969 and 1970. In January, there was an overall relative decline in production of 162,584 yards (an assumed extension of the lower production in 1969). In the succeeding months, coincident with the introduction of trained cutter-backtenders, there was a relative increase in production, continuing until July. In July and August, the relative production rate was poorer than in 1969. This was coincident with Alpha's summer vacations at which time the plant was shut down, allowing senior employees their vacation, and allowing for maintenance of the machinery. It was a two-week lay-off for new employees who were not eligible for vacation time.

In October, relative production was observed to be poorer in 1970. These declines were coincident with the hectic solo trial periods for print trainees. Thereafter, production gains through November and December were relatively high. In 8 of the 12 months, 1970 production rates were higher relative to the same periods in 1969.

The resultant gain in yardage for 1970 was 1,329,988 yards, or a 3.5% gain over 1969. In monetary terms, Alpha made approximately $.04 per yard in profit (above costs). The resultant yardage gain was worth $53,199.52.

Outcome in Lamination

The data for lamination is tabled in the same format used for printing (see Table 8.7). Four lamination operators were trained and began to function in mid-July after the summer shutdown. The lamination table groups together production data for two of Alpha's laminating machines, all shifts.

Comparing 1969 with 1970, it may be seen that productive efficiency was equivalent. However, when the subtotals for each six-month period are isolated, it can be seen that production fell off after

June 1969, and continued at this lower rate until after July 1970, when the losses were recouped. Again, these positive findings were coincident with the influx of program graduates into their new production positions.

Because the overall gain of 1970 compared to 1969 was small, 8,641 yards, no major increase in dollar value was realized over 1969. Comparing early 1970 (pre-trainees) with late 1970 (post-trainees) indicates a relative *loss* of 45,000 yards in early 1970 which moved to a cumulative relative *gain* of 36,000 yards for the six months ending December, 1970. In other words, 81,000 more yards were produced in the latter part of 1970 to "catch up" with the 1969 production figures.

Summary

The importance of this chapter lies in the finding that both the quality and quantity of production increased. Turnover declined. While the actual profit gains were not totally attributable to the program, an *additional fiscal resource* was achieved.

Examination of turnover rates indicated an overall 9% reduction over the previous year. These improvements were attributable to the 19% lower turnover rates of those in the upgrade program. Correlated with the introduction of upgraded employees into production, there was an improvement in productivity and in the quality of the product produced. This increase in productivity amounted to a 3.5% increase over Alpha's previous yield, amounting to approximately a $53,000 gain (above costs).

Table 8.1
TURNOVER RATES: ALL HIRED
(First Six Months, 1970)

	All Hired	1-3 Weeks	1 Month	2 Months	3 Months	4 Months	5 Months	6 Months	Stay (6+)
					Terminations				
Jan.	30	3	7	1	3	1	2	1	12
Feb.	25	5	6	3	7	1	1	na	2
March	23	5	6	4	2	2	na	na	4
April	33	13	9	1	3	na	na	na	7
May	27	5	7	2	na	na	na	na	13
June	17	3	7	na	na	na	na	na	7
July	25	5	na	na	na	na	na	na	20
Total	180	39	42	11	15	4	3	1	65
%	(100)	(22)	(23)	(6)	(8)	(2)	(2)	(1)	(36)
Cum %		(22)	(45)	(51)	(59)	(61)	(63)	(64)	

Table 8.2

TURNOVER RATES: SUB-TABLE, NON-TRAINEES

(First Six Months, 1970)

	All Hired	1-3 Weeks	1 Month	2 Months	3 Months	4 Months	5 Months	6 Months	Stay (6+)
Jan.	17	2	6	0	3	0	0	1	5
Feb.	18	5	4	3	3	1	0	--	2
March	11	5	3	1	1	1	0	--	0
April	23	9	7	0	1	--	--	--	6
May	18	5	5	2	--	--	--	--	6
June	16	3	7	--	--	--	--	--	6
July	16	4	--	--	--	--	--	--	12
Total	119	33	32	6	8	2	0	1	37
%		(28)	(27)	(5)	(7)	(2)	(0)	(1)	(31)
Cum %		(28)	(55)	(59)	(65)	(68)	(68)	(69)	

Terminations

Table 8.3

TURNOVER RATES: SUB-TABLE, TRAINEES

(First Six Months, 1970)

	All Hired	1-3 Weeks	1 Month	2 Months	3 Months	4 Months	5 Months	6 Months	Stay (6+)
					Terminations				
Jan.	13	1	1	1	0	1	2	0	7
Feb.	7	0	2	0	4	0	1	na	0
March	12	0	3	3	1	1	na	na	4
April	10	4	2	1	2	na	na	na	1
May	9	0	2	0	na	na	na	na	7
June	1	0	0	na	na	na	na	na	1
July	9	1	na	na	na	na	na	na	8
Total	61	6	10	5	7	2	3	0	28
%	(99)	(10)	(16)	(8)	(11)	(3)	(5)	(0)	(46)
Cum %		(10)	(26)	(34)	(45)	(48)	(53)	(53)	

Table 8.4

TURNOVER RATES: PRE-PROGRAM, PREVIOUS YEAR

(First Six Months, 1969)

Terminations

	All Hired	1-3 Weeks	1 Month	2 Months	3 Months	4 Months	5 Months	6 Months	Stay (6+)
Jan.	42	13	10	3	6	1	2	2	5
Feb.	25	6	9	3	2	1	0	na	4
March	28	5	11	2	3	2	na	na	5
April	22	9	4	1	1	na	na	na	7
May	18	9	6	1	na	na	na	na	2
June	21	9	5	na	na	na	na	na	7
July	29	9	na	na	na	na	na	na	20
Total	185	60	45	10	12	4	2	2	50
%	(100)	(32)	(24)	(5)	(7)	(2)	(1)	(1)	(27)
Cum %		(32)	(57)	(62)	(69)	(71)	(72)	(73)	

Table 8.5

SUMMARY: TURNOVER RATES IN PRODUCTION ONLY

(Cumulative Percent Terminating)

All Terminations

	All Hirings (N)	1-3 Wks.	1 Mo.	2 Mo.	3 Mo.	4 Mo.	5 Mo.	6 Mo.	Stay (6+)	Improvement over 1969
1969, All New Hires	(185)	32	57	62	69	71	72	73	27	
1970, All New Hires	(180)	22	45	51	59	61	63	64	36	9%
1970 Trainees	(61)	10	26	34	45	48	53	53	46	19%
1970 Non-Trainee	(119)	28	55	59	65	68	68	69	31	- 3%

Table 8.6

ALL PRINT MACHINES

(Yards Printed in Thousands)

	1969			1970 gain			1960 gain	
	Standard	Actual	Difference	Standard	Actual	Difference	Actual	Cumulative
Jan.	4,078	4,017	-61	3,499	3,275	-224	-163	-163
Feb.	3,626	3,235	-391	3,702	3,584	-118	273	110
March	4,014	3,842	-172	3,261	3,472	+211	383	493
April	3,283	3,303	+19	3,954	4,039	+85	66	559
May	3,352	3,059	-293	3,297	3,412	+115	408	967
June	3,958	3,705	-253	3,093	3,005	-89	164	1,131
July	2,992	3,132	+140	2,052	2,024	-28	-168	963
Aug.	3,917	3,899	-18	3,143	3,092	-52	-33	930
Sept.	5,287	5,062	-225	3,115	3,083	-32	193	1,123
Oct.	3,728	3,663	-65	3,647	3,522	-124	-60	1,063
Nov.	3,283	3,091	-192	2,947	2,876	-71	121	1,184
Dec.	2,889	2,560	-329	2,752	2,569	-183	146	1,330 [a]
Total	44,408	42,569	-1,840	38,462	37,953	510		

(a) Actual yards 1,329,988

Profit @ $.04/yd. = $53,199.52

Table 8.7
ALL LAMINATORS
(Yards Laminated in Thousands)

	1969			1970			1970 Gain/Loss	
	Standard	Actual	Difference	Standard	Actual	Difference	Gain/Loss %	Cumulative %
Jan.	627	712	+ 85	436	510	+ 74	-11	-11
Feb.	618	705	+ 87	449	544	+ 97	+ 7	- 4
March	746	876	+ 130	529	642	+ 113	-17	-21
April	723	862	+ 140	767	898	+ 131	- 8	-29
May	612	743	+ 131	652	754	+ 102	-28	-57
June	597	681	+ 84	646	743	+ 97	+12	-45
July	436	498	+ 62	688	749	+ 60	+ 2	-47
Aug.	585	681	+ 62	551	651	+ 100	+ 4	43
Sept.	817	941	+ 96	655	781	+ 126	+ 2	42
Oct.	601	708	+ 107	912	106	+ 146	+39	3
Nov.	542	659	+ 117	552	642	+ 89	-28	31
Dec.	404	488	+ 84	588	695	+ 106	22	9[a]
Total	7,307	8,555	1,248	7,427	8,667	1,239		
Sub-totals Jan.-June, 1970	3,923	4,579	656	3,480	4,091	611		-45[b]
Sub-totals July-Dec., 1970	3,384	3,976	592	3,948	4,576	628		+37[c]

(a) Actual yards = 8,641.   (b) Actual yards = 45,216.   (c) Actual yards = 36,575.

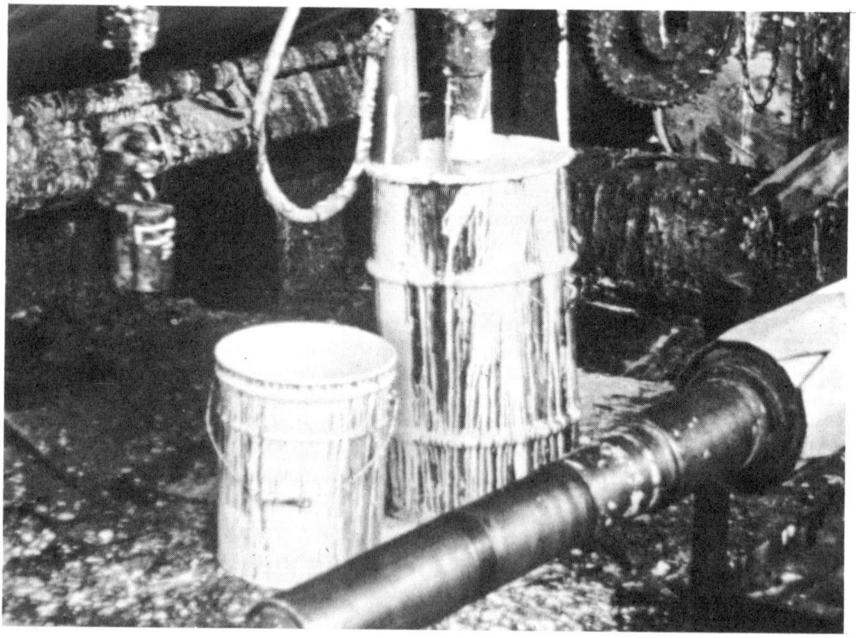

9
Long-term Follow-up

One year later,[1] the records at Alpha were reviewed, and interviews were held with employees, middle management and company President. A number of changes occurred over this long interval.

The company had weathered its "fiscal crisis" but, at one point, had to cut the salaries of middle managers 10%. Its economic prospects for the year (1971-2) were favorable. It had obtained a contract to produce over a million yards of printed vinyl for a large corporation. Sales and sales projections for the first six months (1972) were up.

In the early part of 1971, the General Manager had resigned, following his failure to get a renewal of his five-year work contract under favorable terms. He left to form his own company in a non-related field.

A new three-year union contract[2] had been negotiated in July, 1971, calling for hourly increases of $.25 for the first year; $.15, the

---

1 Long-term follow-up status as of 10/1/71, actually 15 months. For three month short-term status, as of 10/1/70, see Chapter 7.

2 The old contract covered a two-year period.

second; and $.05, the third. The new contract also called for improved pension rights.

As of the time of the follow-up, there were fewer familiar faces. Although they had stayed long enough to complete cutter-backtender training, they had presumably left to find jobs paying more than they were earning at Alpha. The company had not increased their wages, as promised, beyond their initial increments. Of the 8 men in this category, 7 left Alpha for other jobs. The 1 remaining employee in this group had moved into the position of a tuber, earning relatively more than before, $103/wk compared to $86/wk at the three month follow-up.

Of the three new employees who entered *GED Only*, 1 had returned to school as of the time of the short-term follow-up. The others remained at Alpha, both working as tubers or tuber helpers, earning $93/wk and $107/wk, respectively. (They were earning $86/wk and $84/wk, respectively, at three-month follow-up.) Neither had completed GED and the wage gains were not directly attributable to the upgrade program. The gains occurred mainly because of the $.25 raise called for in the new union contract.

Disposition of Printers

Of central interest to this study is the subsequent disposition of the printers. A series of "critical incidents" occurred which are very informative of the status of upgraded printers. Some background events will provide the necessary context for understanding the findings.

In March 1971, all middle managers' salaries were cut 10% as part of an economy move. At about the same time, Alpha arranged to bring back to the New Brunswick plant 1 foreman and 4 printers who had left in 1968. This decision to bring these men back related to several factors:

1. The future sales picture remained poor (as of that date), and a more concentrated effort to bolster sales was put forth, requiring a reorganization of responsibilities and assignments which included most front office personnel.

2. The President took a more direct hand in plant operations and sales, perhaps as a consequence of the announced resignation of the General Manager.

3. The President strongly announced his intention to increase productivity to force a reduction of poor quality outputs as part of the company's required response to its sales crisis.

4. The President made it clear that he was bringing in a new management team to "get rid of dead wood." (The foreman who returned did so on the basis that he would assume operational control of the plant as the Print Supervisor. This meant that he picked his own team of printers, the men who had left with him three years before.)

By April (1971), the "new" foreman had returned to Alpha and the repatriated printers were placed on the presses as cutter-backtenders (at printer wages). Up until that time, 7 of the 14 upgraded printers had been printing on a regular basis for almost 6 months; 3 had been functioning as substitute printers, on and off as needed; and 4 had been promised print positions but were still awaiting promotion to this position.

After working as cutter-backtenders for two months, the Alpha management attempted to place three of the repatriated men as printers. This would have displaced upgraded employees and placed them in the lower wage position of cutter-backtender. Both senior and upgraded printers objected. The union representative was called, because there was a clear violation of their union contract. The company had certified the program participants in the solo trial period and written letters attesting to their upgraded status. The company could not reduce their wages. However, the union contract did not constrain the company from reassigning men, as needed, as long as the higher wage rate was retained and the replacements were also certified printers.

The company proceeded, first, to assign the repatriated printers from cutter-backtender to printer positions and shifted the upgraded printers (program participants) to the support positions of cutter-backtender. The men retained their wage irrespective of their assignments.

Second, the 7 employees in interim status (printer substitutes or awaiting printer openings) found themselves subject to increased pressure; there was detailed scrutiny of their work. "If they didn't like it, they could leave," the print supervisor told them.

Five of the 7 left Alpha, believing the company would not give them the raise and/or promotion it had promised. The last 2 were planning to leave and were looking for jobs as of the follow-up date.

The union representative had told them that nothing could be done about it and to be careful.

The displacement effort was not confined to the subgroup of new upgraded employees. It also included 2 of the 3 upgraded senior employees as well. One man subsequently left, the other was transferred to cutter-backtender. The third man avoided getting caught up in the reshuffling, because he was on assignment to the laminating department during this period.

All told, 8 of the 14 initially upgraded printers remained after one year, working in back-up or substitute printer positions. These men also increased in wages because of mandatory contractual increases of $.08/hr. in December, 1970 and $.25/hr. in July, 1971. The current (as of the follow-up) and initial (pre-program) wage rates are shown in Table 9.1.

Table 9.1
Wage Increments, Printers Wage

Trainee No.	Initial Wage (Pre-program)	Current Wage (10-1-71)	Wage Increase	Percent
3	100	143	43	43
28	100	143	43	43
36	84	123	39	46
45	132	152	20	15
58	100	143	43	43
110	84	110	26	31
112	84	143	59	70
136	84	123	39	46

These critical events point up some latent benefits and limitations in the upgrade program.

1. The ability of the remaining printers to hold onto their job is related to the company and union's recognition of their upgraded status.

2. The printers were more able to avail themselves of union protection than employees who had not received full recognition.

3. The new men were not treated any differently by the company. The same displacement occurred for senior employees who were upgraded.

4. The failure of these men to protect their seniority over the returning printers was an inherent weakness in the union contract and the representation they got from the union.

5. While their morale has been negatively affected by these events, they were tenacious in trying to retain their wage scale and expected to be asked to print again. It was doubtful that this response would have been elicited if they remained solely in entry-level status.

6. It will take time before the company will place as much confidence in rapidly upgraded employees as it does in printers who acquired their skills as a consequence of long-term apprenticeships. Even though upgraded employees produced satisfactory goods, the company views the repatriated foreman and his four printers as better qualified to increase productivity and raise work quality.

7. The company is reluctant to use the upgraded men as printers because it may stir up the displacement issue again. Consequently, it is not likely that they will stay with the company unless the situation changes.

Of those 6 printers who left or were forced out, 5 could be located in a field follow-up. All had found other jobs quickly. They were in jobs paying more than Alpha, but the jobs were not as printers. One man was in car assembly work at Ford Motor Co., 2 were in construction jobs in Florida, 1 was working for Public Service as part of a street repair crew. In all of the new jobs, the men were at the lower rungs of the promotion ladder.

Disposition of Operators

Of the 4 upgraded lamination operators that had completed the program, 3 were working in the lamination department, 1 had terminated. The remaining 3 men had increased earnings as mandated by the new union contract. These wage increments are shown in Table 9.2.

Table 9.2
Wage Increments, Lamination Operators

Trainee No.	Initial Wage (Pre-program)	Current Wage (10-1-71)	Wage Increase	Percent
81	99	122	23	23
109	103	126	23	22
114	131	148	17	13

Wage Increases

As expected, the wage data for upgraded employees indicate that most wage benefits accrued to those who could be promoted. It is of interest to examine the relative gains made by newly hired and upgraded employees in contrast with their pre-Alpha job status. These data are shown in Table 9.3.

The data indicate that most have exceeded their previous wage status, some with considerable wage gains.

Plant Atmosphere

At entry level, Alpha was continuing to experience very high turnover. For example, according to company records, some 53 employees terminated or were terminated over the three-weeks just prior to the follow-up visit to the plant. Given Alpha's total work force of 150 blue collar workers, this was considered a high figure. Of the 53 employees, 10 were in lamination (19%), 20 in print (38%), 16 in extrusion (30%), and 7 in the warehouse (13%).

The manifest attitudes of production supervisors and personnel with regards to these entry level employees had not changed over the period of time Alpha had been studied.

The opinion of the President was of interest. Aware of the high turnover, he felt that he was better off now, having increased the flexibility of the production department in terms of his trained employees. His view of the high turnover was that it was a minor cost, because productivity was up and the per-man wage costs relative to production had gone down. (His views are covered in greater detail in the next chapter.)

He explained the turnover of the non-printer employees as being the result (a) of their not being disciplined workers, (b) of their poverty backgrounds, (c) of some discriminatory behavior on the part of foremen, and (d) of their need for more experience which he could not afford to give them.

Summary

The data presented indicate that most (57%) of the upgraded printers held onto their jobs and increased their wage benefits.

Several upgraded employees had been dislodged from their jobs as printers while others had left as a result of a managerial reorganization of the production area. This factor together with Alpha's negative plant atmosphere and the company's failure to meet all its commitments produced serious morale problems for these employees.

While still experiencing high turnover at entry level, the company did not feel that this was a serious cost element because of the influx of trained and upgraded employees.

Table 9.3
WAGE CHANGES RELATIVE TO LAST PRE-ALPHA JOB
(Printers Only)

	1 Yr. Status	Previous Job Position	Weekly* Wage	Academic Skills	Alpha Wage	Differences in Wages	Percent
3	Stay	Helper	$100	5.8	$143	$43	43
28	Stay	AC Refinish	145	5.8	143	-2	-1
36	Stay	Service work	90	5.6	123	33	37
64	Leave	Printer	76	8.6	113	37	49
110	Stay	Assembly	100	6.8	110	10	10
112	Stay	Helper-labels	128	6.6	143	15	12
116	Leave	Helper	84	9.0+	110	16	19
127	Leave	(Army)	na	5.3	113	na	na
131	Leave	Janitor	40	8.4	120	80	200
133	Leave	(Army)	na	7.6	113	na	na
136	Stay	Maintenance	65	7.4	123	58	89

* Reported weekly wage; not confirmed.

10
Policy Findings, Upgrade Conditions and Variables

Introduction

Many policy questions, issues and upgrade variables have been discussed in earlier chapters. In summary, this chapter considers the conditions and variables observed in one company which may effect upgrade programming in a wider range of settings.

Absence of Displacement Concerns

When training unemployed workers directly for skilled jobs in companies where there are large higher skill shortages, displacement risks tend not to occur for the reason that there is sufficient promotion space. In a small firm such as Alpha, where there was concurrent upgrading of new hires and senior employees, there was sufficient promotion space in higher skill openings, and, therefore, displacement concerns were not manifest. In fact, new employees did occupy higher skill positions over senior employees who did not participate in the upgrade program. Neither the contractor's staff, management or the union reported any such concern on the part of senior employees.

In terms of wage differentials, new employees caught up to and exceeded those of some senior employees. Senior employees were observed to be more concerned about immediate wage differentials than specific job progression mobility ladders with deferred long-term gains in wages. Notwithstanding the fact that mobility is directly related to how much money the worker could earn, senior employees largely elected not to participate. The company's history of poor employee relations may have been a factor discrediting any belief in long-term wage gains.

In this respect, even the higher wages earned by upgraded new employees over senior employees were not viewed as a form of displacement and provoked no concern on the part of senior employees.

There are several factors, observations and suppositions that may be advanced to explain the absence of displacement concerns on the part of senior employees.

1. Senior employees were offered the same mobility routes and elected not to participate. Consequently, they acceded to the possibility of new employees being upgraded over them. They either thought it would not occur, did not believe the company would meet its obligations, or did not think the differential benefits were worth the effort that would be involved. In fact, all of these attitudes were present, perhaps the most important being the insufficient wage benefit differentials.

2. The union contract, in an institutional sense, can be viewed as a system of fair rules regarding who and how any employee can be upgraded. Since new employees were upgraded by the rules of the union contract, senior employees (not trained), by these same rules, were ineligible. The process was viewed by senior employees as legitimate, not as a subject of criticism or reproach.

3. Because they were earning wages higher than new employees, the economic status of senior employees was not threatened by the promotion of new hires to a position higher than theirs. Even after new employees were upgraded, their wages were not significantly higher.

4. New employees had become "old" employees by the time the project was completed. In effect, new hires became the *majority group* because turnover continued to reduce the number of senior

employees (as had been Alpha's experience in the past). As members of the larger group, their opinions colored the company atmosphere as regards displacement. They were, in effect, the displacing group, and did not view the process negatively.

5. Both new and senior employees were of minority group status and no interracial conflict among co-workers existed at this specific site. Promotion of Blacks did not lead to any racial stress.

6. Senior employees of higher skill status (printers and lamination operators) were already at the top of their progression ladders, earning more than upgraded employees. As such, they were not economically threatened or superseded in their occupational status.

7. Other blue collar departments, such as the warehouse, employed large numbers of low wage employees. It was physically removed from the production areas and the program. The warehouse was viewed as having its own separate progression system. Changes in the production area did not effect it. If warehouse employees were interested in changing over to production, they could enter the program. They chose not to participate, and, consequently, no displacement threats accrued.

8. New employees were not subsidized over senior employees. Rather, the program development and contractor's operations were subsidized. New hires came in at the same low wages as had been true for senior employees. Release time was paid by the company, but it was available to senior employees as well. (For example, they did utilize release time for GED.) The program did not subsidize one group of workers over another.

In sum, while new employees were able to fill positions normally available to senior employees only, displacement concerns on the part of senior employees were not observed. This occurred because there was: concurrent upgrading, agreement to abide by the contractual arrangements for upgrading in the union contract, lack of highly differentiated company wage levels, similarity in ethnic composition of blue collar workers, and avoidance of direct differential subsidization of new employees.

Resolution of Employer-Employee Needs

In the demonstration, attention was focused on the relationship between the problems and needs of the employer and those of the worker, particularly the least skilled. Accommodations between these two "needs" areas potentially serves as a foundation for the adoption of an upgrading system. Given these issues, it is relevant to consider the employer's reasons for participation.

Employer Rationale

What factors affected Alpha's decision to incorporate, as part of its manpower development plan, an internal upgrading system?

When Alpha decided it was not possible to go into the labor market to hire the highly skilled labor necessary to advance its productive capability, it turned to other methods. Few alternatives were left to them. Raiding other companies could only be of temporary advantage. The productive system could not be automated to eliminate the printer. Apprenticeship training was not tried, probably because there were so few instances of employees working themselves up to higher skilled jobs.

At Alpha, it was not possible to dilute the printers job so that lesser skilled employees could operate the presses. The low margin of profitability did not permit any lowering of the quality of goods produced; consequently, the situation was economically threatening.

Technical capability in job redesign and training was not part of Alpha's experience or expertness. The research into upgrading by the contractor meshed with its need. After assuring itself that it could not be economically hurt by obtaining a sub-contract to cover additional training expenses and additional operational costs, it was prepared to go ahead with the project.

The objectives of the company, as stated earlier in this report, were its desire:

1. To increase production and increase profits;
2. To fill skill shortages;
3. To reduce quality of workmanship, especially in attaining first quality goods; and
4. To reduce high turnover.

The project proported to meet these needs.

Employer Assessment

In assessing the project in these terms, it can be seen to have had some degree of success. It was greatest in meeting its objectives in improving production and in improving quality of workmanship and resolving skill shortages. It met with less success in producing a sustained decline in turnover. While turnover declined 19% among participants, it was apparent that employees did continue to leave if at a slower rate. While these latter turnover returns are not totally assignable to program (given the factors of company-employee relations and its low wage levels) in the viewpoint of company management, it did not want to be persistently strained by a consistent influx of new employees. It looked toward the program as a solution to this problem.

An upgrading program must prove itself to the employer by producing results in its specifically specified areas of need. It is important to observe that "needs" in a small company such as Alpha, in long-range planning, are largely seen in terms of future sales and low cost purchases of materials, as well as in the need to give priority to better quality assurance methods (post-product sampling) rather than quality control methods (supervisory and employee monitoring of production). Its need is primarily viewed as maintaining and increasing production, in close supervision without commensurate improvements in work stations. It considers employee morale to be less of a company responsibility than an attribute of the men the company is forced to hire for entry level jobs. The viewpoint and appraisal of Alpha's president are of interest insofar as they reflect this point of view.

Retrospectively, the President considered the upgrade program to have been of value. He reported that he was planning to obtain a NAB/JOBS contract for entry level training and upgrading into extrusion operator.

In his appraisal, the most negative aspect of the program was its "lowering of the morale of first-line supervisors," and, secondarily, the inability of the program to control some men "who were undisciplined workers and did not want to get ahead." The most positive aspects of the program was its ability to enable Alpha to obtain both sufficient printers and to have trained print employees as backup men for cutter-backtender positions. He did not object to paying the higher wage scale, since these men were of potential use to the company. He reported the company's economic prospects as favorable; they could support these costs (in 1971). He did not know whether newly hired printers or present printers would stay with the company and felt that he could not control who stayed or left, but he now had a cushion.

As to future profitability, he viewed the new management team as moving strongly in this direction. The previous purchasing agent was replaced. A new quality assurance program was being planned, and the labor costs per-running-foot of goods printed was at an acceptable ratio.

By implication, this criteria meant that there had been a sufficient increase in productivity to offset increased wage costs. There was a continuing high rate of turnover in entry level positions. As long as these costs did not substantially cut into the company's profit picture, it was viewed as having a lower order of priority to the company.

It may be conjectured that as long as the company was producing a profitable return for its operations, when small costs accrued as a result of turnover, it was accepted as "a cost of doing business."

The company's interest in a NAB/JOBS contract derived from its plan to expand the extrusion department through the purchase of an additional extruder. The additional extruder was justified by Alpha's increased productivity and improved sales picture. It would not entertain, currently, its own internal financing of entry level training but would do so under NAB/JOBS.

The above opinions and reflections of Alpha's President leave open the question of why Alpha elected not to continue the upgrade project on its own. This is discussed under institutional changes.

Employee Participation

In part, the demonstration asked: "What would be the resultant composition of the company's internal labor force? Which employees would choose to participate?"

Alpha's history of employee relations with both mid-level and entry level employees was always characterized by mutual distrust. Conflicts invariably arose over such issues as: how much money should have been in the pay envelope for overtime hours, delays in receiving agreed upon wage adjustments, whether the employees were working or loafing, lateness and plant conditions. These factors impacted upon the mid-level employees willingness to participate in an upgrade program because they were distrustful of company motives in establishing such a program.

Of concern to senior employees was their fear of loss of seniority rights should they fail the program. The company had to indicate that this would not occur and that the union supported the upgrade program. These concerns were even pronounced among employees that the company relied upon. For example, a barrier to obtaining the consent of three Alpha employees to serve as OJT trainers was their fear that they would lose their positions as printers or operators. A wage bonus, offered by the company, was of lesser interest than written assurance from the company that they would hold their job titles, seniority and could return to work as printers or operators. They also insisted that the union be party to the negotiation. When all three elements (bonus, written assurance and union surveillance) were agreed upon, they consented to participate. (Even then, the company did not pay any bonus for several months although it had promised to do so. When the company did pay the bonus, retrospectively, the men complained that they were short changed on the effective date of the agreement and were not given what was promised. It took several weeks to straighten this out.)

Mid-level employees did not believe that the company would make good on its promise to promote successful trainees. The fact that senior employees participated mainly in GED classes, not skills training, attests to their degree of interest in upgrading programs. There were no monetary benefits to be earned from participating in the GED program, and there was no potential threat of losing seniority rights.

One conclusion that can be drawn from these observations is that the matter of seniority rights and assurance against threat of job loss must be taken up during pre-program negotiations and be made part of the program specifications acknowledged by both the company and the union.

Wage Differentials

Mid-level employees completing the upgrade program, because of their longer tenure with the company, could not receive significant wage increases. This wage differential was an important factor underlying their general lack of participation in the program. They were interested in promotion to the first step of another job ladder. If the employee was at the top wage step of his job position, the wage differential was not sufficiently greater. This problem was especially pronounced for mid-level employees who have earned bonuses above union scale because of their exemplary or longer-tenured work performance.

To encourage more senior mid-level employees to participate, it was necessary for the company to promise to start the upgraded employee at a higher wage scale than the beginning union scale paid for these new positions. Only with these adjustments, given Alpha's wage scale, was it possible for the mid-level employee to exceed the wages he was already earning.

These observations point up the need to provide for sufficient wage differentials and to develop these wage guidelines so as to not disenfranchise employees who have proven themselves to be good employees. This may turn out to be a formidable problem in a small firm because of greater constraints in wage and profit margins. In Alpha's case, it is important to note that in its particular relationship to the union, union scale was frequently below actual wages paid to senior mid-level employees

These factors would seem to suggest that other firms would have to regulate the amount of upgrading it could support, as well as whom they would select to participate in the program. In any case, wage differentials are an important element to consider before initiating an upgrade effort.

Paid Release Time

The provision of release time, paid for by the company, was a basic requirement for getting employees to participate. It is doubtful that employees would have done so on their own time, in this specific company, because of the length of time involved in training for upgrading, the relatively low wages paid by the company and its history of poor employee relations.

Release time made it possible for employees to receive an upgrading input. They would not have participated otherwise. Without release time, even senior employees would not have participated. However, even the provision of release time did not insure that the employee would complete the program.

Finally, the providing of release time (paid for by the company) added credibility to Alpha's expressed interest in upgrading.

Commensurate Wage Increases

One outcome of the demonstration was the finding that upgraded employees did receive wage increases commensurate with their increased skills and promotion. Although these increases were less than promised, it demarked a change for a company known in the area for paying low wages.

Because of the initially low wage, some of the increases were substantial, 40% more. As noted, these increases were below those originally promised by the company. Most wage increases occurred for those completing the full upgrade program, for it was those employees the company judged to be the men it wanted to retain.

In Alpha, the union contract wage scales were below those paid to many of the employees. This feature of the contract permitted Alpha to differentially reward its employees.

In larger firms, where contractually fixed wage scales are more characteristic for blue collar workers, the employer would be obligated to fully meet the wage commitment.

Employee Experiences

An index of the range of new experiences and concerns faced by the new hire, as identified to staff, is of interest. They help define the kind of stress an employee experienced. These data are derived from project notes and memos, tallied and ordered as to frequency of occurrences in two contexts: the factory floor and the classroom. The data given below identify both conflicts with the company, ever present confusion about rules and regulations, concern about progress in the program, and doubts about the sincerity of the company.

Factory Floor

Issue	Frequency	Percent
Employee accused of not telephoning when absent; he says he did[1]	13	12
Employee confused about vacation allotment during periodic shutdown	12	11
Employee upset about not having enough practice time printing	9	8
Employee upset about delay in transfer to print department	9	8
Employee sick and wants to leave floor	9	8
Employee fired by foreman	9	8
Employee plans to quit company and drop program	8	7
Employee complains money missing in pay check	8	7
Senior employee wants explanation of why not accepted into GED	7	7
Employee not paid for lost time due to injury	6	6
Employee wants to be rehired by company (after firing mainly)	6	6
Employee threatened by co-worker	4	4
Employee wants to drop program and return to former department	2	2
Foreman cursed employee	2	2
Employee reported to wrong shift, not allowed to work	2	2
Employee playing with pay check of co-worker	1	1
TOTAL	107	(99%)

1 This is a cause for firing.

Classroom

Issue	Frequency	Percent
Employee doubts sincerity of company	29	27
Employee complains about OJT trainer having favorites	14	13
Employee complains about ineffectiveness of union	12	11
Employee doubts sincerity of training program	9	8
Senior employee "bugs" new employee	8	7
Employee doubts sincerity of trainer (Skill)	8	7
Employee complains classroom pace too slow	6	6
Employee wants to know if he gets paid if he resigns	6	6
Employee complains about being constantly watched by foreman	4	4
Employee inquires about procedures for leaving the plant early and what if foreman says no	3	3
Employee questions retirement benefits of company	3	3
Senior employee complains about receiving the same increment as new worker	2	2
Employee makes a disapproving remark relative to the religion of a peer	1	1
Employee leaving state for better job	1	1
Employee complains that crew members don't obey him because of his youth	1	1
TOTAL	107	(100%)

Employee Discipline

It is important to place the difficulties inherent in accommodating and developing a larger group of new hires in perspective. Consequently, a similar index of issues, as identified by the trainer, is presented. These data indicate that there were work and training discipline problems, of varying degrees of "seriousness," with some employees. These factors were expected and were not especially pronounced in the experience of project staff.

Trainer Difficulties

Issue	Frequency	Percent
Employee continually absent from class (print)	15	18
Employee not following work procedures	12	14
Employee not retaining information	11	13
Employee reluctant to read aloud in class	6	7
Employee harrassing female staff	6	7
Employee not reporting difficulties	6	7
Employee overly playful in class	5	6
Employee sleeping in class	5	6
Employee not following safety procedures	4	5
Employee not utilizing supportive services	4	5
Employee reluctant to speak English in class (Spanish)	3	4
Dropping participant (laxity)	2	2
Dropping participant (lack of ability)	2	2
Physical handicap	2	2
TOTAL	83	(98%)

Foremen and Supervisors

Critical to the success of the project was the participation of the first-line supervisory staff and foremen. Except for 3rd shift personnel, they were brought together to go over program details prior to the start of the program.

Most of the details on the development of the program and instructional materials had been developed without their involvement. As a means of involving them, they were solicited for their inputs to the manuals being produced in the printing and laminating-embossing departments.

These occasions were intended to serve the purpose of informing and gaining advice as regards the operation of the program and especially to win the full support of the foremen for the project.

The presentations were company sponsored. The General Manager gave them the objectives and expectancies which led the company to agree to participate. He told them what he expected in the way of their efforts.

The contractor discussed the role of the trainer, the team itself and detailed what should *realistically* be expected from new employees. For example, if new employees were not yet trained to change press coppers, they should not be asked to do so until the training had been completed. Schedule difficulties and the priority given production requirements were emphasized, balanced against the need to train employees.

In the subsequent course of the program, their experience indicated that there was a need for continuous vigilance, otherwise the men ruined all production schedules. The difficulty in getting out the work was mainly centered with new employees, some men who once worked up to par, and one or two printers. It was their contention that trouble makers had to be weeded out. For example, one foreman said: "Many of the men don't care; they are unable to keep or appreciate jobs, highly argumentative and goofed-off whenever no one was looking." He believed, "One had to be fair, give the man a chance, but not get the stick yourself."

As regards the program, they accepted it but did not believe it would really change things. They were never won over to the program. Getting ahead by improving one's skills required more motivation than they saw in these new employees. It was their contention that success was dependent upon the individual. If he wanted to do it, he could.

In part, the attitudes of the foremen were racial. The most adamant were those in print production. All the foremen in this unit were whites who had transferred to New Brunswick when the company shifted its operations from Trenton. The other two foremen, in lamination-embossing, were Black and were highly supportive of the program. They had also transferred in from Trenton.

One foreman's attitude was sufficiently obvious so as to require his transfer to the night shift as a disciplinary move because of his bigotry. According to the President of the company, "That straightened him out. He changed and we transferred him back."

In part, the negative behavior of the foremen was provoked by trainees "hasseling" them, explaining that they had to get off production because they were scheduled to go to class. Of course, some employees were discipline problems. They excused their work behavior by referring to their "special" program status.

The foremen were also caught in the middle of managerial production demands and low employee morale. The employees felt, correctly, that the company had not met its commitments in paying the increased wages on time. The employee wanted improvements to be made as regards rest periods, lunch and toilet breaks. While there are no direct measures of the impact of these attitudes on foremen, it is logical to assume that they felt some of the brunt of these attitudes and some acting-out of felt grievances.

The first-line supervisor had little to gain from the program. It only increased his problems since he was responsible for the quality and quantity of the goods produced. The program design did not provide any incentive for him in terms of any bonus or other benefits.

Notwithstanding the above, behavior and performance ratings of trainees on the floor by the foremen (and the printer and OJT trainer) indicated that most of the men did well.

Foremen were important to the upgrade programs. One employee's view is instructive: "If you don't make it with the foreman, you don't make it."

Program planning in this area must give serious consideration to incentives for foremen and supervisors who are not direct beneficiaries of upgrade programs.

Long-Term Effects of Program

Both follow-ups allowed for an assessment of whether upgrade efforts have long term effects. The short term, three-month follow-up indicated that 74% of the new hires had completed their training and 47% had stayed at Alpha. Nineteen percent of the new hires went on to complete the print program and remained in employment as of the three-month follow-up. In addition, seven of eight senior employees were upgraded to printer or lamination operator.

The long term, one-year follow-up indicated that several of these upgraded new employees had subsequently left Alpha, bringing the percent of upgraded employees (printers) remaining in employment at Alpha down to 10% from 19%. Among present employees, five of the original eight remained. For a small company, these upgrade rates were high and indicated that the upgrade effects were sustained for those who fully completed the program. In contrast, almost all of those who did not complete the program left Alpha. Those separating from the program before completion experienced long periods of unemployment, but subsequently obtained jobs, some of which paid entry wages higher than Alpha's. Those separating after completing the program got jobs readily, probably because they planned for the separation by locating the job, usually at wages higher than they were earning at Alpha. No matter how far they had progressed in the program, all were at the bottom rung of the job progression ladder in their new jobs. The skills learned at Alpha were not directly related to the types of jobs they subsequently found.

The higher wages were attributable to the seasonal character of some jobs (construction), special situations such as working for a relative or better union representation.

The upgraded employees found it difficult to get jobs as printers in another firm for mainly two reasons:

1. Many did not know of other firms performing the same type of work (printing plastics) and were turned away from publishing firms because their skills were not directly transferable without apprenticeship. They rejected apprenticing at lower wages

2. They needed a formal credential certifying the skill and curriculum they had successfully completed. Other employers in the same type of business did not accept their report as to what they learned while at Alpha at face value. In part, this may be attributable

to differences in the technology utilized at other plastic-printing firms. In any case, these employers were unwilling to try the men out on their machines.

Institutional Changes

Entry Level Requirements/Attitudes

Alpha, as a low wage employer, recruited locally from the Black community and accepted men with almost no credential restrictions. The applicant's educational status and his skills (those acquired elsewhere) were generally not considered. The only exceptions were men who could not speak English well. They were generally only hired for non-production jobs.

During the course of the project, the entry requirements were not changed. The main observable effects on entry level employees were the following:

1. A temporary, short-lived increased tolerance on the part of the foremen for "infractions" committed by men in the upgrade program.

2. A positive and increased concern expressed on the part of production management as to the status and well being of new hires. (There were promises to improve work stations when the program was completed.)

3. No apparent change in company disposition (described elsewhere) toward new hires who had not entered the upgrade program. Their turnover rates were the same when compared to the previous year.

4. A complete cessation of complaints by the printers, those which occurred prior to the installation of the program, that they had poorly staffed and trained crew members. There was considerable willingness on the part of printers to help the new man upgrade himself. The printer was not concerned about being displaced or loss in his earnings.

It is important to note that these positive and supportive activities on the part of printers were sustained even though the standard in print production on which increased incentive payments was based had not been exceeded. The marked gain over the previous year was, however, noticeable (see Chapter 8).

In the long run, after the project had been completed, these interim effects tended to have less effect; the pre-program atmosphere largely returned. Nonetheless, because the company had greater flexibility in its skilled manpower pool at program's end, it was increasingly less abrasive toward subsequent new hires (see Chapter 9).

Educational Credentials

The importance of educational credentials was minimal. The job task analysis of work requirements for printers and operators indicated there was a need for extensive skills in mathematics, reading, physics and chemistry. The printer and operator positions did not require a high school diploma. In fact, most of the men successfully meeting printer requirements through the upgrade program did not have a high school education; some could not read very well.

New employees were observed to be least interested in education and opted for increasing their wages as a first step in skills training. Of those eleven new employees who were upgraded to printer, four chose *Mixed* (skills + GED), seven chose *Skills Only*.

Present employees chose GED, but did not do so with a view of being upgraded within Alpha. Even a high school equivalency diploma would not have made for increased mobility within Alpha. There is no data as to their mobility potential with other companies.

In hiring at entry level, Alpha preferred men with a high school background. The employment officer assumed that there were correlations between promotability, ability to learn the job, employee discipline and whether or not the employee had earned a high school diploma. Without regard for the truth or falsity of this assumption, a man with a high school diploma could not go much further than a man without a diploma within Alpha's productive organization, all other things being equal.

It is of passing interest to note that the President of Alpha did not know that a high school equivalency diploma could be earned as a result of passing a state certified test. On learning that the state made such certification, he accepted its legitimacy.

There is no data, in this project, as to whether separated employees with high school equivalency diplomas would have done better in looking for work with this credential in hand. While this problem was of interest to the contractor, the fact that few obtained equivalency diplomas made this aspect of the research unfeasible.

Non-Continuance of Upgrade Project

Upon completion of the project, Alpha recognized that it had undergone a trying, although successful experience. The larger volume of trainees had fostered a higher wage bill. The excess of printers had posed problems of absorption as well as higher wage costs than anticipated. Added to this strain was the more immediate factor of an economic turndown. Sales projections had fallen to a three-month lead time, a level considered perilously low by the company (a 6 to 9 month lead was considered *reasonably safe*).

By September 1970 the national economic turndown had begun to affect Alpha -- as it had other small plants in the New Brunswick area. Sales at Alpha decreased markedly, resulting in a 50% decline in backlog orders. Alpha instituted its first layoff in several years. The layoffs amounted to approximately 10% (6 people in the general helper category) in the print department. The extrusion department had cut back to four days per week. The product mix in lamination was adjusted in order to boost sales (although at a lower profit ratio) and the work in the print department was stretched out over three shifts.

The layoff did not affect any employee-trainee. Layoffs occurred in order of seniority. The employee-trainees in the program were now *old employees*, having been with the company for several months. Those affected were those just hired. They were not members of the union and had no seniority.

The economic turndown affected the immediate upgrading of 4 program graduates. They were delayed or given substitute printer status.

The economic turndown in turn, raised the question of relative costs of the upgrade model as against Alpha's usual method of training new employees.

Costs

At the time of this report, no upgrade training was occurring. New hires were assigned to the printer who "broke them in and trained them." It was assumed that the cost of providing OJT was already subsumed within Alpha's present operating budget. Printers were used as trainers and no release time was used to break-in entry level employees.

In contrast, the upgrade model used to develop employees for promotion to higher skill jobs (i.e., beyond entry level training) would have added additional costs -- in excess of Alpha's present method of training. The upgrade program involved the additional costs of a trainer and the cost of release time. The basic costs were those of salary, approximately $8500 per year per trainer,[2] and release time of $520 per trainee.[3] Assuming Alpha upgraded three printers per year, its costs would come to approximately $10,000 per year, plus add-on costs of production wastage and slow-down for practice. The costs of materials development, job analysis and pilot demonstration were already covered by the upgrade project.

The new program for extrusion or embossing would have increased the estimated cost given above. Education was not critical as an upgrade credential; employees could be selected with sufficient educational skills from among Alpha's senior employees. Since these costs were well within Alpha's fiscal capability, it was only one of several reasons for not continuing the program.

The company also found itself in changed circumstances. It now had more than enough skilled personnel, with reduced turnover at entry level. Several business-like questions follow:

1. Why pay support for a training and upgrade program when it is not needed any longer for developing high-skilled employees?

2. Are the turnover losses at entry level equalized by expenditures in training and upgrading to reduce these losses?

3. Are there offsetting "fringe" benefits to employees which justify the costs of upgrading, such as having relief crews for lunch and rest breaks? Does upgrading improve employee vigilance in protecting against quality control failures?

---

2 The same wage as a starting printer.

3 Eight hours per week, at an average hourly rate of $2.50/hr for 26 weeks, or $520.

Together with the economic factors described earlier, the company decision was to discontinue the upgrade program when the contractor completed its work. Even when the economic picture began to improve in mid-1971, the company could not, and probably would not, have reversed its earlier decision. There were sufficient printers. The OJT trainers had been re-assigned to printer or operator duties. Because of the company's delay in paying them what it had promised (and delays in upgrading them to A printer), the former OJT trainers were angry. They did not want to become involved again.

Even though the company failed to carry on the upgrade effort, it is important to observe that the redesigned cutter-backtender job was not changed. While the boundaries of one job as against another were more diffused, the cutter or backtender had not returned completely to their old duties. The new duties of each crew member in performing the common job of set up and color change was largely retained. This was not solely attributable to the job redesign, since this was an earlier tradition of separating printer and crew functions.

Adoption would have been more readily considered if there had been a precedent for formal training, such as found in companies with training departments. As well, there would have been lower costs of adoption. In considering these factors, it must also be surmised that had there been fewer printers trained over a longer period of time, less strain would have been felt by the company and their absorption capacity would have been better.

Industry-Focused Technology

The project demonstrated that industry-focused techniques, such as job redesign, upgrade models and multi-stepped progression ladders, are feasible in plants with flat occupational structures, and may be used to concurrently upgrade entry level and mid-level employees. The essential conditions for upgrading involve a low ratio of unskilled employees to skilled employees (at Alpha, two cutter-backtenders to one printer), sufficient skills differentiation between lower and higher skill jobs, and sufficient promotion space.

Appendix A
R & D Typology Of Industrial Upgrading Conditions and Variables

I. DESCRIPTION OF THE UPGRADE TYPOLOGY

The research typology attempts to take into account the occupational conditions in which upgrading can occur. Occupational conditions are sub-divided into five related factors: occupational structure, skilled/unskilled employee ratios, skills differentiation, plant (labor force) size, and promotion space.

1. *Occupational structure*, it is generally agreed, delimits the number of job progression steps in an occupational skill category. Three general occupational structures are grossly pictured as pyramidically shaped: (a) extended job structures (where job progression sequences include six or more discernible steps in a job progression sequence), called *long, narrow pyramid*, e.g., in the steel industry; (b) *moderate pyramid* (where job progression sequences range from three to five steps in a promotion sequence), e.g., auto industry; and (c) *flat pyramid* (where job progression sequences are severely limited, usually one or two steps).

Craft occupations depart from this general classification because of their special relationship to occupational structure. Typically, craftsmen are already pre-trained in a vocational school and/or take an apprenticeship. They are usually hired into the industrial pyramid near the top of the progression sequence. They have limited progressions in their occupation, since they are already working in or toward skilled jobs at the outset (i.e., they already have apprentice or journeymen status).

At first view, industries with compressed occupational structures provide a low ceiling for upward movement (as in small or moderate sized industries), because of the limited number of higher skilled positions, while *long, narrow pyramids* are not structurally restraining because of the high occupational ceilings.

To the factor of occupational structure one must add several qualifying exceptions which may enhance or constrain upgrading possibilities.

2. *Unskilled/skilled employee ratios* are a further consideration. If the ratio is large, say, 20 unskilled employees for every skilled employee, the number of employees who may potentially move upward is more severely limited than if the unskilled-to-skilled ratio is, say, 5:1.

In the latter case, 20% of the unskilled labor force could potentially move upward for every vacancy or opening in skilled positions. In the former case, only 5% could potentially move upward. Directly related to this consideration is the factor of skills differentiation within the industry.

3. *Skills differentiation* within the company's blue collar work force affects upgrading opportunities, and may vary widely between production departments within a company. This factor has received little attention in the upgrade literature.

If the work tasks within or between departments are similar to the point where almost anyone can readily acquire and perform the work tasks of other employees throughout the facility, there is no existent upgrading potential. All skills are at the same level and, consequently, there is no upgrade mobility below supervisory levels. Only limited upward movement into supervisory or foremen positions is possible.

However, the presence of separated skill groups within the plant offer opportunities for developing upgrade programs if mechanisms (e.g., training, wage differentials) for interdepartmental movement are created or exist.

Appendix A

4. *Plant (labor force) size* defines the number of people who may be upgraded, as well as the potential number of jobs at higher skill levels. For example, a small plant may organize its labor force into production units of five unskilled employees relating to one skilled employee. In a production plant of 60 people, there are only ten upgrade positions that could become available. In a larger plant of 600 people, there are 100 potential positions.

The above considerations -- occupational structure, skill ratio, skill differentiation, and plant size -- are addressed in the broader question of the number of upgrade positions available in any occupational structure. For purposes of discussion, this factor is termed *promotion space*.

5. *Promotion space* defines the total number of upgrade opportunities available in any plant. Promotion space may be directly calculated or estimated for current or future needs. Elements entering into measuring promotion space include: (a) turnover in high skill positions, (b) skill shortages and unfilled openings, (c) planned expansion of labor force, and (d) changes in manpower utilization. Promotion space also depends upon the extent to which these occupational, pyramidal-shaped structures employ more workers at lower skill levels than higher ones

In the *long, narrow* occupational structure, promotion space includes the number of job positions into which employees could squeeze into at the narrow top, and takes into account the number of steps (job upgrade positions) at *each* level throughout the narrow-shaped pyramid. For example, there may be limited upgrading space at the top but there may be, beyond entry level, sufficiently differentiated job steps at each production level to permit a large, *absolute* amount of upgrading, although relatively decreasing at each progression level.

Upgrade Climate

Upgrade climate includes those considerations related to management and union participation, existent criteria for selection of upgrade candidates, type of training and education, mix of employee-participants, type of upgrading to be utilized, and goals of the industry involved.

1. *Management's* view of the importance and place of upgrading in its corporate planning varies markedly. Management operates, as best it can, in a manner it believes to be most efficient for corporate growth and profit. Companies have established, as part of their historical growth, specific production jobs and production facilities to efficiently turn out its product or service. The procedures it utilizes is, to a large degree, dictated by the type of production methods it employs, the way product production is organized, the company's experience in securing and retaining manpower, the system of seniority affecting existing workers, and the number of fixed job categories. Although these factors promote organizational consistency and stability, they may also act as constraints against change, expecially as they affect the upward movement of its employees.

Changes in upgrading practices may be given greater priority under pressures of skill shortages, requirements to sustain and improve production, employee unrest, opportunities inherent in new plant construction and relocation, and so on.

While upgrading in industry is not a new phenomenon, there is the recurring question as to the place of upgrading in company manpower practices, upgrade methods utilized, technique effectiveness, and cost. In short, the importance of upgrading may well depend on its utility to the company, and this varies widely.

Aside from management motives to participate in an upgrading program, there is also the central question of the degree of support they will give to such an effort. Corporate management's consent and support is a mandatory prerequisite for any upgrade effort. Aside from corporate management, there are the needs and attitudes of line personnel (supervisory) to be considered; i.e., their specified role in upgrading. There is little or no research concerning this managerial group as it relates to upgrading.

Managerial support may be limited or it may not, and this would likely be the case for all levels of management. In the typology, there is a distinction made between these two levels of participatory involvement -- as *limited* or *active*, first, for foremen and supervisors and, second, for production managers (to whom they report).

2. *Union participation and sanction* is another upgrade element. In non-union or company-based unions, managerial discretion as regards upgrading may be far greater than for managements who must account to unions that are part of a regional or national organization. Operationally, unions vary in the way they are involved in manage-

ment decisions, particularly as they affect the union's membership. Some are involved on almost a day-to-day basis while others are involved only in settling employee disputes (when they arise) and at contract renewal.

Union participation and its sanction are important: (a) when such issues as job redesign or change in work stations are involved or (b) when expansion of the bidding system to cover upgrading is involved.

Unions do not typically initiate upgrading programs. They vary in their interest as to the importance of upgrading to their membership. In some unions, it is felt that management has the prime responsibility for supplying the resources (and monies) needed to initiate upgrading programs. Unions generally participate to the degree that they want the right of approval, but only after such plans have been developed by company management.

While union participation or sanction is mandatory, there is wide variation in the degree to which the union actively advocates, promotes and supports such programs. We distinguish between two types of union interest: *continuous*, where upgrading is an active component of union policy; and *focal*, where upgrading is acceptable to its policy and/or practices but the union merely sanctions the program.

3. *Selection criteria* for upgrading vary in different industries, generally determined by the type of union-management agreement. In an industrial firm with a strong union, seniority rules apply in the selection of candidates for upgrading. The longer the employee has worked at the firm, the more it is mandatory that he be selected first for upgrading. Posting and bidding for jobs is the normal procedure in most industries, but selection criteria may vary widely depending upon local agreements. The formal elements that enter into the selection process are: (a) seniority, (b) worker ability, (c) test performance, (d) supervisory evaluation, (e) employee experience, and (f) educational background. In this formal system, differing weights may be assigned to each component in the selection criteria. These weights are computed in a complex manner, with a high degree of flexibility in the amount of leverage the company can exert to gain upgrading for a given group of employees.

The broader issue of who gets upgraded is usually part of the labor-management contract, while the responsibility (including the mechanisms) for upgrading is management's responsibility.

Where seniority alone determines selection, the amount of wide-scale upgrading (including upgrading of entry level employees) which can be introduced is unknown. Typically, seniority is a constraining factor. For example, when jobs are posted and bid, seniority plus the employee's ability (actual or anticipated) are heavily weighed. Where there has been a formal training program prior to upgrading, say, in lower skill jobs for more junior employees, then judgments of the worker's ability may supersede seniority. In plants where some entry level employees have been trained for higher skilled jobs, and consequently have the skills, they may supersede more senior employees who do not have the requisite skills. As indicated, these promotion rules depend upon local agreements and the structure of formal training programs within the company. If training has been made available to both junior and senior employees, both may advance to higher skilled jobs even though other employees with seniority (not participating in training) are bypassed.

There is an *informal* selection system as well. Informal considerations include: (a) the unwillingness of some senior employees to bid for an upgrade position;[1] (b) the company's encouragement or discouragement of senior employees; (c) the concern about changed inter-personnel relationships in upgrade positions;[2] (d) the company's face and concern about discriminatory or restrictive practices which may encourage selective upgrading only among specific employees; (e) the special agreements with the union made for selective programs or positions; and (f) the fact that night or third shifts are usually not bid by senior employees. These events may be sufficiently flexible so that an entry level union employee, say, a porter, may successfully bid for a much higher upgrade position on third shift and receive training for that job.

In general, it is reasonable to assume that an upgrade system, extending from entry level into successively higher skill positions, can provide company-wide routes to higher skill positions, for both employees with junior and senior status if skill shortages exist or are anticipated. On the face of it, most of the data indicate that unions support upgrade efforts especially as they

[1] If he fails, he is not able to try again; he may be embarrassed. When he returns to his old position, he may have to be reassigned to a new crew or supervisor. He may also not want to do harder work.

[2] He may lose old friends; he has a new role (maybe new hours). He has to relate to new people.

Appendix A

relate to union members on a seniority, "first come, first serve" basis. Where promotion is not defined solely by seniority, more opportunities exist for those with junior status and for new hires. It is clear, however, that these arrangements involve management and union consent.

Other firms, by practice, do no internal upgrading but hire in skilled employees, e.g., in hiring tool and die makers. Still other firms may follow a mixed practice of some upgrading and hiring in. This may vary by division, plant, or type of skill shortage.

To distinguish the selection procedures we use the following subclassifications: *seniority bidding, open bidding,* or *hiring in.* Companies may follow more than one such practice.

4. *Training and education* are key mechanisms for promotional advancement. Company practices vary as to the type of training it makes available, and when an employee is to be trained. At entry level, the training is usually informal, conducted on-line (during production) by the first-line supervisors and co-workers or both. Hiring and promotion are based on prior experience or accumulated on-the-line experience.

Beyond entry level, either as a prerequisite for upgrading or postselection for upgrading, the training is usually more rigorous and consists of formal OJT with or without classroom training; it may be conducted by the company's training department. Companies train as needed and do so in response to immediate skill shortages. The quality and efficiency of such training varies markedly. Typically, training departments do not participate in the development of plant-wide programs for either direct skill training or upgrading; they generally do not assume any responsibility for formal on-line OJT. Their domain tends to be restricted to classroom (supportive skills) training, and may include supervisory training and human relations training.

The relative juxtaposition of manual skills to basic or remedial education is the subject of diverse opinion. Ideologically, many companies believe that the more formally educated employee will more readily prove out in acquiring upgrade skills, and will become a reliable and valuable employee. Educational components, supportive of manual skills, may be added to the skill training programs. They may be made a part of the selection criteria for upgrading. However, many blue collar workers possess manual skills with little formal education. Over time, many have risen into higher skill categories and thus have demonstrated, in one sense, that some question exists about the exact place of formal education in an industrial context. The relative need for basic education as a mechanism of the internal or external labor market is, as yet, not fully researched.

We distinguish several types of company training procedures: *classroom program, supervisory training, OJT, job experience only* (no training), and *education* (remedial, basic, or advanced).

5. *Employee-Participants.* Because there is some concern with the requirements set forth by the Equal Employment Opportunity Commission (EEOC), greater interest is invoked regarding the question of who does and does not come to participate in employment and subsequent upgrading. There are several groups of focal concern:

    a. Employed, but low income workers.

    b. Unemployed workers who cannot move into entry level jobs.

    c. Racial minorities under-represented in skilled jobs.

    d. Employees in middle level jobs who cannot advance because of structural, company-based limitations.

    e. Employees in middle level jobs whose job performance is judged to be inadequate and in need of skills improvement.

6. The *type of upgrading* defines the scope or range of the upgrading being practiced (or possible). This may range from entry level through successive skill levels to supervisory or management positions. In most instances, movement upward, say, from semi-skilled to skilled work, creates vacancies to be filled, say, from entry level to semi-skilled. It is a traditional industrial practice.

An upgrade system starts with entry level positions and extends through successive semi-skilled levels to skilled jobs and, sometimes, into supervisory positions. Depending on circumstances it may even extend further -- into redesign of entry level positions for new hires or upgrading from supervisory into management positions.

7. *Industry goals* for participating in an upgrade program may derive from many sources. There are usually multiple reasons involved in a specific company's decision to participate in an upgrade program. These reasons may include: (a) high turnover and absenteeism, (b) poor quality of workmanship, (c) poor worker discipline, (d) skill shortages, (e) desire to increase production and increase profits, (f) anticipated machine redesign or other technological changes, (g) union pressure, and (h) employee pressures arising from worker discontent with wages, working conditions, benefits, or discriminatory practices.

II. Upgrade Program Development

Upgrade programs are a composite of techniques leading to specific models. Both the technique of upgrading and the models which are derived from them are described below.

Upgrade Techniques

Both the occupational structure and the climate for upgrading will impact on the type of upgrade model potentially suitable for the company. Given the combination of factors within the company, a blending and/or modification of existent upgrade techniques is often necessary. A review of some basic techniques follows:

1. *Job task analysis* techniques are used to describe (by detailed observation) the work that has to be done and the tasks actually performed to get the work done. For example, job task analysis (JTA) may first be used to define the job or work sequences by discerning whether tasks are related to (a) handling materials, (b) machine input or feeding materials, (c) machine tending, (d) machine operations or control, (e) crew management, (f) machine output, (g) quality/quantity testing and (h) setting up and repair.

Each of these tasks may be sub-analyzed in terms of level of job difficulty, skills, or educational prerequisites including the time it would take to train. When applied to several levels for purposes of upgrading, JTA provides basic data for: (a) redesigning of jobs, (b) writing of new job descriptions, (c) setting performance standards, (d) establishing skill requirements and employee selection criteria, and (e) identifying training and supervisory needs.

2. *Job fractionalization* is defined as an analytic technique for "breaking down" a complex, skilled job into its component units. Once identified, these units may permit the reassignment (or allow for a new alignment) of job duties and tasks in a redesign model.

This technique may be used to delimit a worker's essential advanced skills from the wide range of duties he actually performs, many of which may not be skilled. For example, a material-flow supervisor may be responsible for the transport of objects and materials, using dollies, hand trucks, and/or fork lifts. He may also be responsible for inventory and maintenance. The skills involved in steering a hand truck and lifting heavy materials, in how to route them quickly through the plant, are of a different order of difficulty than the skills required for systems planning and inventory control.

In an upgrade model, the lower-order skills may be transferred to an upgrade employee-trainee so that he can begin to acquire the duties of the material-flow supervisor or the material-flow supervisor could be further trained in systems planning and inventory control as prerequisite for an upward progression into management.

3. *Employee supports* identifies any requirements to adjust the immediate work environment of the employee (formal and informal OJT, counseling, supportive services, and education); it is relevant to upgrading insofar as it is in support of skills development. For upgrading, it may involve: (a) taking or responding to instructions, (b) exchanging or receiving of information, (c) learning to give instructions, and (d) training a replacement person.

Upgrade Models

The content and focus of most upgrade models is to provide for a spanable relationship from one job position to another. The more fluid the organization of job stations supported by training and/or experience, the more readily upward job mobility may occur. There are several such models, including *job redesign, job progression ladders, job enrichment, job enlargement, through-put, High Intensity Training* and *job engineering.*

1. *Job redesign* involves the development of a new job. It may be developed by fitting two jobs together (collapsing) or separating a higher skilled job so as to form two new job classifications (expansion). For example, in a department with drill press operators where the operator does his own setup, production may be changed to include a separate setup man. The setup man's main job is to put together drill press jobs and test them before a production worker sits down to turn out parts in large numbers.

2. *Job ladders* or job progression ladders involve the sequential ordering of jobs, from low to higher skills, so as to provide a series of promotional steps leading into higher skilled jobs. For example, in a flat occupational structure where there is only a foreman and production workers, the progression of a worker to supervisor may best be routed through an assistant foreman's position.

3. *Job enrichment* involves a change in the content of work performed in a specific job so as to promote motivation and prerequisite experience for advancement to a higher skilled job. For example, movement from shop assembly to field or customer services may, in terms of knowledge, require that the employee also diagnose what is wrong in the functioning of a machine. Job enrichment may require that the employee rotate through (or spend time in) the test laboratory to gain this diagnostic know-how; subsequently, he would be eligible for promotion.

4. *Job enlargement* involves a change in the scope of work performed for the purpose of generating a high quality grouping of skills. For example, it may be desirable, in order for the company to maintain quality work performance and manpower flexibility, to require multiple rather than unitary skills. Consequently, the job requirements may be enlarged so that, say, a welder specialist can perform and qualify in several welding processes rather than one only.

5. *Through-put* refers to upgrading where one outcome may go beyond internal upgrading (promotion within a company) to also include external upgrading (advancement to higher level openings at other companies). Where occupational constraints completely limit upward movement, the present plant may be a staging area for the employee to move up, but out of the company. The trade-off for the company may include longer tenure, better quality of work, less employee dissatisfaction, and a fluid labor force

6. *High Intensity Training (HIT)* is a short duration (usually 40 to 60 hours) intensive training program geared for small skill jumps directed toward a specific job-change position. It is a practical and utilitarian training technique which promotes upgrading.

7. *Job engineering* attempts to establish an efficient and logical sequence of job stations. The stations are sufficiently overlapped in skill requirements so that the learning of one job simultaneously prepares the employee for the next. He may "slide" into each successive skill level, with little training, from one position into another of higher order because of the close proximity of one job station to another.

In the course of future work, it will be necessary to consider and append to these basic models other upgrade models that best suit the differences which obtain for different work-force organizations.

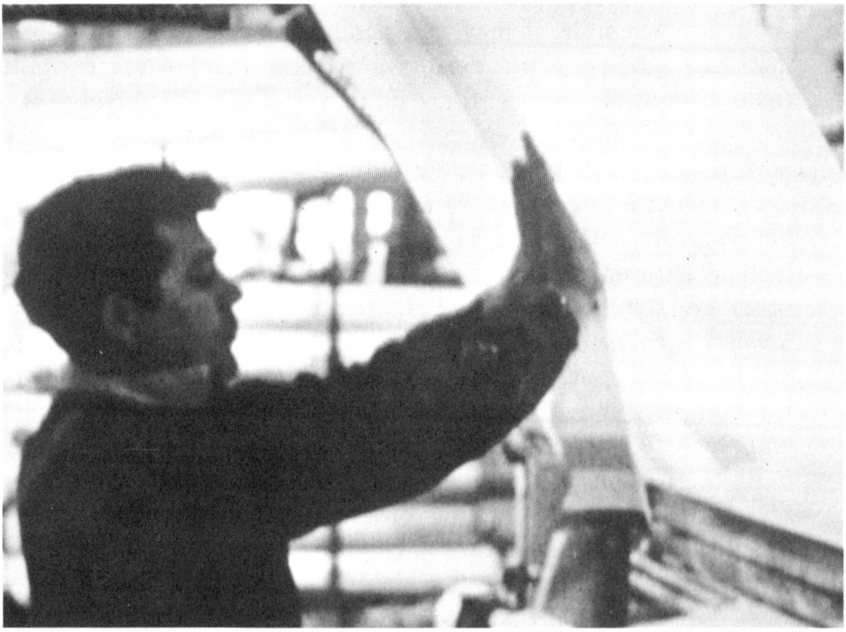

Appendix B
Supportive Services

Introduction

When this study was first conceptualized, the contractor assumed that the employees recruited from the ranks of the unemployed would, in contrast to senior employees, be subject to special pressures by virtue of their prolonged unemployment. The contractor hypothesized that these new employees would experience garnishee assessments, need money to pay his medical bills, have food and residence needs, and, possibly, have need of legal assistance. It was also possible that these men might experience difficulty in moving into their new status as skilled members of the labor force. As such, upgraded employees might require special assistance during this transition; he might need consumer education, day care for his children; and he might need to learn about the educational facilities and social service agencies in the community. He might also need housing assistance and help in budgeting his money.

In point of fact, actual field experience dictated that these apriori preconceptions were questionable. Specific supportive service components were reexamined. The results indicated:

1. Applicants for jobs were not unemployed for excessive long periods of time and did not use up Unemployment Insurance benefits.
2. Many applicants were working at another job while exploring employment at the company.
3. Many applicants were single.

As an alternative mode, a more basic research stance was adopted, setting as its initial objectives two priorities: (a) an empirical identification of the problems brought forth by the employee-trainees (problem identification) and (b) the empirical identification of problems which would or could be handled within an industrial context (problem resolution).

Methodology

Data Collection

All program participants received an informing interview from the supportive service staff. The interviewer described the objectives of the supportive service program as offering legal and referral services, personal counseling, financial and family assistance. These services were available on an *as needed* basis, and employees could avail themselves of these services, free-of-charge, as they saw fit, at any time.

In the weeks that followed initiation of the program, periodic inquiries were made of participants as to their possible needs, reminding them of the availability of these services. They were canvassed individually for any problem they cared to identify. The staff did not *solicit* the trainees for problems. Each problem, when identified by the employee-trainee, was taken "first come, first serve" and thereafter pursued as far toward resolution as possible. Records were kept describing the problem, the type of effort involved, the monies spent, and the time involved.

Services

The supportive service counselor acted within certain general boundaries. Where possible, the resolution of the problem was handled as if on direct assignment to the personnel department of the company. In effect, the counselor attempted to provide services that could have been administered out of the personnel department in a normal (non-program) manner.

In preparation, a list of community agencies and services was developed. The eligibility requirements, application procedures, and names of agency personnel to contact were prepared in advance. A local lawyer was made available on a retainer for advice and referral. Both a social worker and a psychologist were "on call" if assistance was needed.

Analysis

Definitions

The operational definitions of supportive services included those services which were necessary for the reduction of non-training related problems, those faced by the trainees that would conceivably affect their employment and/or training status. For example, a trainee facing jail for lack of early legal advice would be lost to the program. As such, supportive services were defined as activities (listed above) which attempted to alleviate problems that might have jeopardized the trainee's employment status. In this sense, all problems catalogued below are "work related," since all had very high likelihood of interfering with the trainee's work on the factory floor or with his training or both.

In practice, there were grey areas in defining these problems which affected employment. For example, a man who experienced mood shifts which, in turn, created an irritation among his co-workers, might or might have not moved in the direction of more severe altercations with co-workers. However, when he threatened to fight another worker, then the employment status of both employees was in jeopardy. These grey areas often appeared in areas of marital-family problems, paternity, and family desertion. In these areas, unless there was an instance of threat of loss of employment, the problem was not counted as "work related."

Treatment of the Data

Each problem identified is counted as a single separate problem. For example, if an employee-trainee required money for a lawyer, the problem was counted as a legal problem, not as legal and monetary. However, if the trainee required a lawyer and also needed housing, two distinct problems were identified, and each is counted. These are considered multiple problems.

A few instances were difficult to count for one or another reason. The choice made is indicated, as follows: (a) *lawyer for a domestic quarrel,* counted as *family;* (b) *family desertion because of alcoholism,* counted as *alcoholism;* and (c) *no money for a place to stay,* counted as *needing temporary housing.*

A classification system was used to summarize the data. First, problems were classified into six categories which describe what was needed to resolve the problem.

1. *Inability to purchase services* because trainee did not have sufficient money, e.g., pay rent.
2. *Services available in community but not known or utilized* by employee, e.g., family counseling center.
3. *Referral recommendations only* because problem could not be handled by the contractor, e.g., addiction.
4. *Problems requiring services from individuals with specific knowledge for expertness,* e.g., immigration problem.
5. *Problems requiring counseling,* e.g., conflict with co-worker or supervisor.
6. *Problems which require long-term social service follow-up,* e.g., paternity.

Second, problems within each category were classified as to the degree of success achieved. Four outcomes are recorded.

1. *Resolved,* which indicates that the contractor was able to handle the problem, using its own staff personnel and resources. The problem was resolved without referral.
2. *Referral accept,* indicating that a *successful* referral was made, i.e., the client was accepted for service by an appropriate agency in the community.
3. *Referral reject,* indicating a failure because a referral could not be achieved (e.g., agency was overcrowded) or beyond the financial means of the employee (e.g., psychological help).

Appendix B

4. *Couldn't help,* indicating that there was no service available or client refused to go.

Findings

Fifty-eight percent of the trainees, both new and senior employees (N = 40), were identified as having one or more problems which were work related, while 42% of the trainees were problem free.

The high percentage of problem-free employees points up the fact that most of the employees felt they could deal with their own difficulties without staff assistance. Even those who identified their problems had in the recent past taken care of problems of similar magnitude themselves. Nevertheless, there are critical periods when the employee needs interim assistance to deal with an immediate pressing problem.

The distribution of problems for the 69 employee-trainees[1] was as follows:

Trainees Report	N	%
No Problems	29	42
1 Problem	14	20
2 Problems	17	25
3 Problems	9	13
Total	69	100%

Table B.1 provides an overview of these different problems, the type of approach they required and the degree of effectiveness which was encountered in dealing with them.

The 40 employees identified 75 separate problems. When these problems are classified, as indicated above, 57% are found as not satisfactorily resolved. They involved problems of providing special educational services *(Classification II);* services requiring referral to

[1] Fifty-eight new employees in skill training, three in G.E.D.; and eight senior employees in advanced skill training.

specialists for drug use, alcoholism and psychological disturbances *(Classification III);* and employee problems requiring long-term social service assistance *(Classification IV)*.

Successful resolution occurred in 43% of the problems. Most were in legal services (staff supplied the lawyer), in housing and in need for immediate money *(Classification I)*. In specialized intercession, such as immigration problems and racial conflict *(Classification IV)* moderate success was achieved. In problems requiring counseling *(Classification V)*, the immediate crisis was often met and mollified; however, staff resources and skills were limited and could not fulfill the need for intensive counseling. The approach used was to offer guidance and counseling; this was followed by referrals to agencies for follow-up services.

An analysis of the data, identifying specific problems derived from this field experience with Alpha, indicates:

1. One garnishee problem was encountered.

2. Problems related to consumer fraud, consumer education, and day care services were expected, but none were identified.

3. A relatively high rate of narcotic usage was encountered (16% of all problems), while alcoholism, homosexuality and apparent psychological disturbances accounted for an additional 13% of all problems. Taken together, these problems were not dealt with by the staff because of lack of skills or resources to deal with them.

There are two points of particular note in attempting to supply supportive services:

1. Many trainees were unaware of available community services. However, even when trainees were informed of available community services (with offers of transportation and personal assistance), very few utilized or attempted to avail themselves of these services.

2. Social service agencies offer services for which there are relatively few openings. Where openings are available, high fees are charged, as in child care programs. The Adult Basic Education (ABE) and English as a Second Language (ESL) programs are not operating locally. Also, some of the agencies have long waiting lists, as well as complicated application procedures, as in the case of the Rehabilitation Center and the Veterans Administration. In addition, many of the local agencies were uncooperative to the point where they would not even furnish the staff with a description of the kind of service they offered.

Appendix B

Finally, it cannot be said that the provision of supportive services reduced entry level turnover although it did slow down the rate for some employees. It can be said that there may be a protective element insofar as supportive services protect a training dollar investment in an upgraded employee. For example, of the eighteen fully upgraded employees,[2] some eleven employees had been serviced, mostly by counseling, referral to legal assistance, and by family agency referral.

Summary

Several guidelines suggest themselves based upon the program experience and data collected.

1. Many employees did not utilize supportive services or perceive a need to do so. They preferred to handle problems by themselves (42%).

2. Of those that identified problems, some 57% were not resolvable either because there was no such service in the community, the agency could not accept the referral, the employee refused to go, or the problem required long-term services. Particularly resistant problems from the perspective of gaining treatment services were: drugs, alcoholism, homosexuality, and psychological disturbances.

3. Some 43% of the problems identified could be served. These areas include: (a) legal assistance, (b) counseling, (c) specialized intercession, and (d) referral to community agencies. Many of these areas lend themselves to an industry-based service in the sense that they can be administered and coordinated within the operations of a personnel department, provided there is a staff person available to carry out these activities.

One of the major problems in supplying supportive services was the large amount of time required by the staff to service clients. Initial interviews of trainees and follow-up on their behalf, even the process of finding the proper sources for trainee referral, consumed much of the counselor's time. In addition, new cases continually increased the workload.

4. Unless effective administrative procedures are created to handle trainee problems, it proves very difficult to anticipate problem areas

---

[2] Fourteen printers and four laminator operators.

and deal effectively with them. Ultimately, a wide variety of referral agencies, but relatively little financial support, are required to service a wide range of trainee problems.

5. Relatively low costs are incurred in servicing these areas, excluding staff wages. Legal assistance can be secured when needed at a low, per-individual cost (or by retainer). More ready access to community agencies for employees can be secured by a company that contributes to such general community welfare funds as the United Fund.

6. There is some indication that supportive services did not markedly reduce turnover at entry level, although it did tend to protect a training investment in the company's upgraded employees.

7. Though it would appear to be feasible, much more research work is required to develop a workable, low-cost industry-based supportive service model to demonstrate its payoff to the company in terms of greater morale and reduced plant conflict as a protection of the company's training investment in an employee.

Table B.1

SUPPORTIVE SERVICES: PROBLEM IDENTIFICATION

(Multiple Problems)

Classification I: Inability to purchase services

	Resolved	Referral Only Accept	Referral Only Reject	Couldn't Help
Legal Services (N=13)				
Legal advice	7			
Court appearance, jail	5			
Garnishee	1			1
Housing Resources (N=5)				
Inability to pay rent	1			
Needed temporary housing	4	4		
Financial Resources (N=1)				
Immediate (emergency) need for money	1	1		

Table B.1 (Cont)

SUPPORTIVE SERVICES: PROBLEM IDENTIFICATION
(Multiple Problems)

Classification II: Services available in community, not known or not utilized

	Resolved	Referral Only Accept	Referral Only Reject	Couldn't Help
Educational Services (N=6)				
Adult Basic Education	1			1
English as a Second Language	5			5
Medical Services (N=2)				
Speech pathology	1		1	
Physical rehabilitation	1		1	

Classification III: Referral recommendations only

Narcotics Use				
(Referred, Would Not Go) (N=11)				
Known users, suspected interference with work	3		3	
Other suspected users	8			8

Table B.1 (Cont)
SUPPORTIVE SERVICES: PROBLEM IDENTIFICATION
(Multiple Problems)

Classification III: Referral recommendations only (Cont)

	Resolved	Referral Only Accept	Referral Only Reject	Couldn't Help
Alcoholism (N=3)				
Coming to work drunk	2		2	
Drinking on job	1	1		
Homosexuality (N=3)				
Interferes with co-workers	1		1	
Non-interfering, but annoying	2		2	
Psychological Treatment (N=3)				
Manifest behavior problems	3			
	1			2

Classification IV: Problems requiring specialized expert intercession (N=8)

Immigration	1	1		
School-work schedules	3			
Inter-racial conflict	2			

Table B.1 (Cont)
SUPPORTIVE SERVICES: PROBLEM IDENTIFICATION
(Multiple Problems)

	Resolved	Referral Only Accept	Referral Only Reject	Couldn't Help
Classification IV: Problems requiring specialized expert intercession (N=8) (Cont)				
Discrimination in housing	1			
Finding job commensurate with education	1	1		
Classification V: Problems requiring counseling (N=9)				
Frequent inter-personal conflict with co-workers	7			
Fear of machinery	1			
Frequent mood shifts	1			
Classification VI: Long-term social service follow up (N=11)				
Family conflicts	8		7	
Paternity	3	1	2	

Appendix C
General Education Development
(GED) Program

Introduction

The education program was structured as a sub-experiment within the upgrade demonstration project. A job task analysis of the advanced skill position of printer and lamination operator indicated that the upgraded employee needed to be able to work with numbers, fractions, division, rate and percent computations; he also needed to read and evaluate performance charts. Some knowledge of physical chemistry was needed, especially pressure and heat, viscosity and temperature, chemical solvents and elasticity.

To enhance the employee-trainee's ability to work with the training manuals and to be able to read technical articles, support in basic educational ability was required.

The decision to move beyond a program of basic education to one offering the potential of passing a high school equivalency (GED) was predicated on two main assumptions:

1. A GED program could subsume the necessary basic educational requirements of training and also provide the employee with an equivalency diploma.

2. Senior employees would respond more readily to a program that had the potential of a diploma since many had not completed their high school education.

The GED program was structured (a) to provide basic education and (b) to specifically target an objective of his passing the State's GED examination, without attempting to fully supplement what may have been missed by the men because they did not enter or complete high school.

The research questions of major interest were:

1. Would both new and senior employees equally participate in the program?

2. Would employees in the program advance sufficiently to pass the State's high school equivalency examination?

3. Would the occupational mobility of new employees, if they should leave the plant, with or without advanced skill training, be enhanced if they had the "credentials" of a high school equivalency diploma?

Description of GED Test

The High School Equivalency Examination, also called the General Education Development Test (GED), covers five major high school subjects. The certificate is awarded by the State of New Jersey[1] solely on the basis of successful examination completion, regardless of school grade attained prior to leaving high school. The means of acquiring the classroom training needed to pass the examination is not specified. There are five tests:

Test 1: *Effectiveness and Correctness of Expression.* Main emphasis is upon ability to avoid errors in spelling, punctuation, capitalization, and grammatical usage.

Test 2: *Interpretation of Reading Materials in Social Studies.* Main emphasis is upon ability to read with understanding (comprehension) and to critically evaluate reading sections concerning social, political, economic, and cultural problems.

Test 3: *Interpretation of Reading Materials in Natural Sciences.* Places its main emphasis on scientific vocabulary and a background

---

[1] The same requirements apply in most other States and territories.

of information concerning important scientific topics, laws of nature, and scientific developments.

Test 4: *Interpretation of Literary Materials.* Focuses on special abilities not frequently subject to interpretation in ordinary reading materials, such as the ability to interpret figures of speech, to cope with unusual sentence structure and word meanings, and to recognize mood and purpose.

Test 5: *General Mathematical Ability.* Focuses on ability to solve problems of a practical nature -- life insurance, installment buying, taxes, investments, simple home construction and repair projects -- as well as ordinary arithmetical skill and reasoning ability. It does not go into higher mathematics, but includes some elementary algebra and a little geometry.

State Eligibility Rules

Anyone who was *not* graduated from an approved high school may become a candidate for the Certificate provided he meets the following minimum requirements:

1. Age:	Minimum age, eighteen years and out of school for one year
2. Residence:	Applicants must be residents of the state
3. Education:	No previous attendance in high school is required
4. Exam. Scores:	Applicant must attain satisfactory scores in the GED Tests

Satisfactory Score

The candidate must make an average standard score of 45 or more on the entire battery (the sum of the five test scores must equal at least 225) with no standard score under 35 on any one of the five parts of the battery of tests. The highest score made in any one of the five tests in either the original test or the retest is recognized for the issuance of the Certificate. In case the candidate does not meet these requirements, he may find it advantageous to retake the entire battery, particularly if his average score was below the minimum of 45.

In cases where the applicant scored an average of 45 or more but had a score in one test that was less than the minimum of 35, it would be necessary for him to retake only the test where his score was less than 35.

Design of the GED Program

In the planning stage, staff members took the GED examinations, analyzed available GED materials and interviewed staff and project directors of ongoing GED programs.

Based on these data, the following program design evolved:

Program Item	Written at Grade Level	Instructional Hours
Diagnostic Lessons	4 - 6	10
Social Sciences	6 - 8	30
Natural Sciences	8 - 10	30
Understanding Literary Materials	9	20
English Usage	9	20
Mathematics	8	50

1. *Basic education*, as well as educational skills required to support advanced skill training, was incorporated within natural science (physical chemistry), mathematics (fractions, percent, rate computations), and supported by practice and instruction in interpretating written materials.

2. *GED skills* to pass the examination did not require the program participant to know the subject in advance of taking the test. He needed to know how to read, and from that reading to be able to identify specific information to answer the questions. A participant could pass with a minimum score if he possessed this capability. To

obtain a better score, he had to interpret the selection rather than to seek a specific answer. The ability to use the information formed the basis of about one-third of the questions; the remaining questions were centered on the participant's reading background and on classroom instruction.[2]

3. *Homework was eliminated.* The program was structured for self-test reviews so that the instructor could correct mistakes, explain materials and provide immediate answers.

4. *Program limitations,* in terms of eligibility, were necessary since the program was designed for participants having a 6th grade (testable) reading comprehension level.[3] Some participants were taken with a fifth grade level since many of those who applied at Alpha fell into this lower category.

5. *Program Content.* The material selected was similar to that generally encountered at the high school level of understanding and interpretation. The mathematics and natural science units contained information and materials of direct utility for higher skills achievement. Table C.1 lists all lessons in the units which comprise the GED program.

Program Operation

The GED program was offered either alone, without skill training for those interested in trying to obtain a high school equivalency degree *(GED Only),* or in conjunction with skills training for cutter-backtender, printer or lamination operator *(Mixed).*

[2] The recommendations of the American Council on Education -- the national organization which sets the standards for the equivalency examination -- generally supports the judgment of many reading specialists that students who read at the 9th grade level (or above) are capable of comprehension without assistance. That is, their information indicated that the student could pass the tests covering natural science, social science, and literary materials (to a lesser degree) if his reading comprehension was at the 9th grade level or better. See especially, Newsletter No. 31, Commission on Accreditation of Service Experience, American Council on Education, May, 1969.

[3] Students were tested using the Stanford Achievement Test (paragraph meaning).

GED was provided off-site at the Training Center located near the plant. The employer had provided for paid release time for employees in skills training or education or both. Participants were expected to attend class at least four hours a week and no more than eight. If they were involved in *GED Only*, they were expected to attend eight hours. If involved in both skill and GED training, they attended both sections on an equal time basis for a total of eight hours.[4]

The average class size consisted of ten or less participants. They were provided with ring notebooks, pencils, and a paperback copy of the Merriam-Webster dictionary. Lessons were distributed one at a time for insertion into a ring notebook. The participant was expected to move from one set of units to another when the instructor was reasonably sure that he understood the material. The latter, in part, was based on the results which obtained from taking the test at the end of each lesson.

Findings

Differential Participants

Of the thirty-one employees that entered the GED program, 17 were new hires and 14 were senior employees. There were markedly different program preferences between senior employees who selected *GED Only* (10 of 14, 71%) and new hires who selected *Mixed*, GED + Skills (14 of 17, 82%).

As between new and senior employees, the differences in the type of program selected relates to a lesser interest expressed by senior employees in skills training. For example, only 8 senior employees elected to enter skills training. It may be assumed that senior employees, earning more than new hires, did not perceive there to be any advantage to them in taking skill training since it would not appreciably increase their income. They do value education as witnessed by their higher enrollment rate Even so, many of these employees would not have taken GED if the employer had not provided paid release time.

---

[4] The eight hour total for training was provided on company time. The student was given one-half hour before the session to clean up and get to class, and one-half hour at the end of the session to travel back to the plant. The total time spent in class each week was six hours; travel and clean up, two hours.

Appendix C

In contrast, new employees did find it more advantageous to learn the skills of the new job and to thus earn additional income. For the same reason, they also participated in education.

Initial Comprehension Level

The initial educational attainment grade level (reading comprehension) of both new and senior employees was found to be low. As shown in Table C.2, of the total group, 32% scored *less than* sixth grade in reading comprehension, and an additional 29% scored below seventh grade. At best, some 70% of the new hires were below seventh grade compared to 50% of the senior employees. Among new and senior employees, there were many who read below sixth grade in comprehension; and, as such, were considered to be functionally illiterate.

Initially, in designing the program, it was assumed that those below sixth grade would not be able to win a diploma within the time parameters of the program. It was hoped that those participants might be able to gain something in reading, mathematics, and natural science that would be of benefit in the skills training component of the program.

Attrition Rates

Attrition rates were high. Fifty-eight percent dropped out of the program. The reasons for termination as between new and senior employees differ. New hires, because of their more tenuous status with the company, were expected to drop out of the program more frequently than senior employees. Seventy-one percent of the new hires terminated compared to 43% of the senior employees (see Table C.3).

For new employees, termination from GED was the result of difficulty with the company; either being fired or quitting (see Table C.4). For senior employees, it reflected a dissatisfaction with either the employee's rate of progress, the program, or the effort required. Most of the terminations occurred under 60 instructional hours, i.e., in the early phase of the program. This was probably related to the amount of effort involved. There were two known exceptions: one trainee who felt he should have progressed more after 73 hours and one who dropped because of prolonged illness (see Table C.5).

Educational Gains

Fifteen participants were measured in reading comprehension on a pre-post basis.[5] The average grade level gain was 1.2 grade levels for an average of 68 instructional hours. At this rate, 1 grade level per 57 hours was attained by the group as a whole (see Table C.6).

Three variables were selected for further analysis: (a) *GED Only* versus *Mixed* (GED + Skills), (b) initial performance level and (c) senior employee versus new hire. The size of the group limited the type of analysis that could be performed on the data. Only one variable classification could be analyzed.

No differences were found between senior employees and new hires in rate of gain (number of hours for 1 grade level gain). The rate of gains is directly related to the initial grade level scores. The lower the score the longer it takes in instructional hours to achieve 1 grade level gain. For those at fifth grade, 126 hours; for those at sixth grade, 50 hours; and for those at seventh grade, 42 hours. (See Table C.7.)

Those in *Mixed* gained faster than those in *GED Only*. Initial scores are equivalent between groups. The greater rate of gain of the *Mixed* group is attributed to possible motivational differences.

GED Examination

As shown in Table C.8, two participants passed the GED test and were awarded high school equivalency diplomas. The inability of others to pass the examination is largely related to the fact that it was not possible to log sufficient hours as required by the program.

Only minimal success can be claimed by this aspect of the GED program. Since few passed the GED examination, it was also not possible to research the question of whether the employees would have differential mobility as a consequence of earning a diploma.

---

[5] Because of varying instructional hours, due to scheduling, absences and type of participation (GED ONLY or MIXED), the retest period varied.

Appendix C

Summary

Finding 1. Both senior and new hires participated in the education program but for apparently different reasons. New hires did not consider GED as important as skills training and only elected GED together with skills training.[6] In contrast, senior employees elected GED rather than skill training. When electing GED without a subsequent promotion or incentive, they terminated because of the "unrewarded" effort involved.

Finding 2. The program was successful in improving basic skills at a rate of 1 grade level gain for every 57 instructional hours.

Finding 3. Educational programs are intrinsically prone to suffer from high attrition rates because of their long-term time requirements.

---

[6] Although not presented in this section of the report, it is important to note that among those new hires who completed print training only 4 of the 11 were in the MIXED group.

Table C.1

GED PROGRAM

(List of Lessons)

Unit One:	READING THE NEWSPAPER		Grades 4-6	10 hrs.

Lesson

I	Reading Today's News
II	Checking Out the Weather
III	Looking For a Favorite
IV	Looking For a Job
V	Bodies Without Heads
VI	Scrambled Paragraphs
VII	More Scrambled Paragraphs
VIII	Still More Scrambled Paragraphs
IX	Learning to Answer Questions

Unit Two:	SOCIAL SCIENCE		Grades 6-8	20 hrs.

I	Declaration of Independence
II	A More Perfect Union
III	Jacksonian Democracy
IV	The Industrial Revolution
V	The American Civil War
VI	Mass Production
VII	Labor Unions
VIII	World War I
IX	Failure of the League of Nations
X	Nazi Germany
XI	Immigration

Unit Three:	NATURAL SCIENCE		Grades 8-10	30 hrs.

I	Principles of Sound
II	Evolution
III	Structure of the Cell
IV	Heart and Circulatory System
V	An Electric Circuit
VI	Basic Principles of Electricity
VII	The Nature of Gases
VIII	The Solar System
IX	The Laws of Heredity
X	Elementary Chemistry
XI	Elementary Physics

Table C.1 (Cont)

GED PROGRAM

(List of Lessons)

| Unit Four: | UNDERSTANDING LITERARY MATERIALS | Grade 9 | 20 hrs. |

Lesson
- I   Forms of Literary Material
- II   Understanding Poetry
- III Understanding Drama

| Unit Five: | ENGLISH USAGE | Grade 9 | 20 hrs. |

- I   Understanding the Sentence
- II   Parts of Speech
- III Punctuation
- IV   Correct Usage
- V   Spelling
- VI   Test Series

| Unit Six: | MATHEMATICAL SKILLS | Grade 8 | 50 hrs. |

36 units

- I   Concept of Unity
- II   Beginning of Fractions
- III   Fractions & Equivalent Fractions
- IV   Finding Common Denominators
- V   Reducing a Fraction to Lowest Terms
- VI   Adding Fractions
- VII   Reducing Improper Fractions to Mixed Numbers
- VIII   Converting Mixed Numbers Into Improper Fractions
- IX   Adding Complex Fractions
- X   Subtracting Fractions
- XI   Subtracting Complex Fractions
- XII   Multiplying Fractions
- XIII   Multiplying Complex Fractions
- XIV   Dividing Fractions
- XV   Review Problems in Fractions
- XVI   Decimals
- XVII   Working With Decimals
- XVIII Addition and Subtraction of Decimals
- XIX   Multiplication of Decimals
- XX   Division of Decimals
- XXI   Converting Decimals Into Fractions
- XXII   Converting Decimals Into Fractions

Table C.1 (Cont)

GED PROGRAM
(List of Lessons)

Unit Six: MATHEMATICAL SKILLS Grade 8 50 hrs.

Lesson	
XXIII	Working With the Decimal Fraction
XXIV	Rounding
XXV	Percentages
XXVI	How to Work With Formulas
XXVII	Transposing Terms in Formulas
XXIX	Working With Tables
XXX	Squaring and Cubing
XXXI	Geometric Forms
XXXII	Squares
XXXIII	Triangles
XXXIV	Circles
XXXV	Geometric Applications
XXXVI	Graphs and Their Interpretation

Unit Seven: APPENDIX A (ANSWERS)

Unit Eight: APPENDIX B (OPTIONAL VOCABULARY)

Table C.2

INITIAL READING COMPREHENSION (STANFORD PARAGRAPH MEANING)

(All Entering GED)

| | New Employees |||| | Senior Employees |||| | All Enter ||
	GED Only	Mixed (GED+Skill)	N	%		GED Only	Mixed (GED+Skill)	N	%		N	%
			Total					Total			Total	
5.0 - 5.9	1	4	5	29		3	2	5	36		10	32
6.0 - 6.9	0	7	7	41		2	0	2	14		9	29
7.0 - 7.9	1	1	2	12		3	1	4	29		6	19
8.0 - 8.9	0	1	1	6		1	1	2	14		3	10
9.0 +	1	1	2	12		1	0	1	7		3	10
N	3	14	17	(100)		10	4	14	(100)		31	(100)

Table C.3

HOLDING RATES IN EDUCATIONAL PROGRAM (GED)

	GED Only				Mixed (GED+Skill)				All Trainees					
	New		Present		New		Present		New		Present		Total	
	N	%	N	%	N	%	N	%	N	%	N	%	N	%
All Enter	3	99	10	100	14	100	4	100	17	100	14	100	31[d]	100
Did Not Complete	2	67	3	30	10	71	3	75	12	71	6	43	18	58
Completed[b]			6[a]	60	4	29	1	25	4	24	7	50	11[c]	35
Passed: GED[e]	1	33	1	10	0	---	0	---	1	6	1	7	2	6

(a) Four with scores above 200.

(b) Completed the program, did not pass GED.

(c) Of 12 trainees completing the program, 1 had previously received his high school diploma and was in the program for refresher only; 4 trainees did not complete and/or take the exam.

(d) Two trainees had previously received their high school diploma and were in the program for refresher only and did not complete the program.

(e) Completed the program and passed GED.

Table C.4
REASONS FOR GED TERMINATION: NEW EMPLOYEES

Trainee No.	Hours In Program	Reason for Termination	Complete Cutter/Backtender
2	6	Joined U. S. Navy	Yes
3	46	Dropped because of work related injury	Yes
13	6	Quit Alpha	No
26	6	Fired by Alpha	Yes
33	3	Dropped, poor attendance	Yes
37	16	Trainee initiated drop	Yes
51	30	Fired by Alpha	Yes
60	20	Quit Alpha	Yes
72	3	Quit Alpha	No
97	3	Dropped, poor attendance	Yes
128	12	Trainee initiated drop	na[a]

(a) GED Only.

Table C.5
REASONS FOR GED TERMINATIONS: SENIOR EMPLOYEES

GED ONLY

	Initial Test	Retest	Hours in Program	Reason for Termination
23	9.0+	na	9	Trainee initiated drop
32	8.6	8.4[a]	73	Trainee initiated drop
43	5.4	7.6[b]	95	Trainee initiated drop

MIXED (GED + ADV. SKILL)

	Initial Test	Retest	Hours in Program	Reason for Termination
17	5.8	6.8	58	Dropped due to illness
45	8.0	na	20	Trainee initiated drop
58	5.6	na	40	Trainee initiated drop

(a) Retest after 64 hours of instruction.
(b) Retest after 72 hours of instruction.

Table C.6

TEST RETEST SCORES: GED
STANFORD PARAGRAPH MEANING, ALL TRAINEES
(Interim Program Test)

Trainee	New/Senior	GED Only/Mixed	Init.	Retest	Gain Loss	Prog. Hrs.
8	S	GED Only	7.4	8.0	0.6	94
22	S	GED Only	6.0	6.8	0.8	141
28	N	Mixed	5.8	6.6	0.8	42
31	S	Mixed	7.4	10.4	3.0	116
46	S	Mixed	7.6	10.7	3.1	17
49	N	Mixed	5.6	7.2	1.6	75
53	S	GED Only	7.6	10.4	2.8	124
54	S	GED Only	5.4	6.3	0.9	101
58	S	Mixed	5.6	5.3	-0.3	78
70	N	GED Only	7.6	6.8	-0.8	10
80	S	GED Only	5.3	5.0	-0.3	63
89	S	GED Only	6.0	9.0	3.0	90
110	N	Mixed	6.8	7.6	0.8	24
112	N	Mixed	6.6	7.4	0.8	24
128	N	GED Only	5.5	6.0	0.5	20
New (N)	6					
Senior (S)	9					
GED Only		8				
Mixed (GED+Skills)		7				
Totals	15	15				
Average			6.4	7.6	1.2	68
1 Grade level/hrs.					1.	57

Table C.7
TEST RETEST SCORES
INITIAL TEST RETEST LEVELS, AND COMPANY STATUS

Classification	N	Mean Init.	Mean Retest	Mean Gain/Loss	Mean Hours	1 Grade/Hours
GED Only	8	6.4	7.3	.9	80	89
Mixed (GED+Skills)	7	6.5	7.9	1.4	53	39
Classification						
5.0 - 5.9	6	5.5	6.1	0.5	63	126
6.0 - 6.9	4	6.4	7.7	1.4	70	50
7.0 - 7.9	5	7.5	9.3	1.7	72	42
Classification						
Senior Employee	9	6.4	8.0	1.6	92	58
New Employee	6	6.3	6.9	.6	33	50

Table C.8

GED RESULTS

(All Trainees Taking The Test)

Trainee	Prog. Hrs.	Exp.	S.S.	N.S.	L.M.	Math.	Total[b]
1	58	48	54	50	51	48	251
8	140	38[a]	45	50	48	46[a]	227
22	187	36[a]	36[a]	43[a]	42[a]	47	200
28	46	34	27	33	25	32	121
31	116	44	40	42	47	33	206
46	170	44	44[a]	51[a]	43[a]	41	223
54	155	25	15	33	28	26	127
80	113	39	35[a]	33[a]	29[a]	30	166
89	136	37	40[a]	50[a]	45[a]	41[a]	213

(a) Best of two scores.

(b) Passing, 225; min. of 35 in each sub-test.

Key:
    Exp. = Correctness and Effectiveness of Expression
    S.S. = Interpretation of Reading Materials in Social Studies
    N.S. = Interpretation of Reading Materials in Natural Science
    L.M. = Interpretation of Literary Materials
    Math = General Mathematical Ability

Appendix D
Job Task Analysis

Introduction

Job task analysis (JTA) is a method of collecting and grouping the work functions of line or staff employees for subsequent interpretations. Job data generated by this approach may be used in a variety of ways, including: (a) setting of job standards, (b) evaluating job performance, (c) establishing certification or qualification procedures and (d) developing or revising job descriptions.

As used in this project, it was employed in the development of an upgrade program, utilizing job redesign techniques. As such, the purpose of JTA was directed toward gathering data for a multi-level job redesign, and for designing job ladders and the supporting training model.

The central focus of the job task analysis was the determination of the scope of the job, including an identification of the skills of the entry level job, those which would enhance or restrain the trainee from learning more than just perfunctory skills. The intent was to determine the order and magnitude of those skills as a means of identifying the repertoire (at least the major components) participants would need in order to move to more skilled positions. To facilitate this determination, it was first necessary to examine in detail the production jobs of the present crew: cutter, backtender and printer. Functionally, the three jobs were as follows:

1. The cutter, one of the unskilled members of the crew, was stationed at the output side of the press. His function was to monitor the flow and quality of the printed product and to cut off completed goods to specific yardage. It generally took Alpha two to four weeks to train a cutter to proficiency. In this period, he also learned to distinguish a variety of printed plastics and how to handle each. This was an entry level position.

2. The backtender, stationed at the input side of the press, fed materials to the device, supplied ink as needed, and checked on the movement of materials through the machine. It generally took Alpha from four to six weeks to train a backtender. This was also an entry level position although more difficult than that of the cutter.

3. The highest position within the print crew was occupied by the printer. He had over-all responsibility for directing the activities of the cutter and backtender. He was responsible for the quality of the product, including accurate register, inking colors, press speed, etc. The printer was the most skilled member of the crew. It was generally reported to take about three years or more to train a good printer.

Early Phase of JTA

As a beginning step, job descriptions for the cutter and backtender (see Tables D.1, D.2) were examined. These descriptions had been prepared three years earlier; as such, at least in part, they were out of date. They did not accurately or completely describe each man's assignment.

Inspection of the job descriptions suggested several general headings by which the two jobs could be contrasted. Specific duties were assigned to each of the job categories for comparative purposes, as follows:

Cutter	Backtender
Recording, Taking Instructions	
1. Able to read dye order	1. Able to read dye order, select correct raw film
2. Check yardage against order	
3. Record yardage on each roll	2. Record raw material input
Cutting Yardage	
3. Cut neatly and quickly, make new wrap on core	4. Proper splice and splice in time
Handling Materials (Off-bearing)	
6. Remove finished roll and stack	10. Mount new rolls correctly
Tending/Adjusting	
4. Adjust tensions	
8. Control film	3. Control position of roll
9. Control spreaders	
13. Place knife without damaging roller	6. Set knife without damage to rolls
	8. Control ink pumps
Assisting in Crew	9. Keep ink feed to nip
10. Assist backtender, input of raw materials	12. Position dams
11. Assist in color changes	13. Add solvents to ink
12. Assist in set-up and roller changes	
Quality Control	7. Assist in color changes
13. Inspect and signal imperfections: border, smears, scratches, damages, registrations, side to variations in color	11. Assist in set-up and roller changes

This comparative summary indicated that:

1. Distinguishing features of the two jobs were: (a) that the cutter was responsible for quality control; and (b) that different tending duties obtained, probably as a function of his physical location around the press, i.e., input or output job stations.

2. There were many similarities in job duties, such as (a) understanding, reading and filling out dye orders, (b) cutting yardage, (c) handling material, and (d) assisting the printer. In addition, the cutter helped the backtender when necessary.

Observations on the Work Floor

The job descriptions were reviewed after the contractor familiarized himself with the plastic printing process. This "input" was supplied by the foremen and supervisors and from an analysis of the available literature. Thereafter, the men were observed at work in their job stations while the press was running, during set-up and color change-over, during several different time periods. (Observations made of the same activities on the night shift when most of the managerial staff members were not in the plant were most helpful.)

Crew-machine Process

The most striking observation was the large physical size of the presses, 100 feet in length. The second important observation was that the machine almost completely dictated what each crew members duties had to be, and their physical separation one from the other.

While the machine was running the work was relatively easy and routine. When there was a new set-up or color change, the whole

Appendix D

crew had to be involved, sometimes supplemented by the production manager. They were required to complete the complex changeover quickly and without error or damage to the raw materials and the equipment (especially the copper rollers which were expensive and take a long time to repair).

Skill Levels

In all instances, job skills at the entry level (cutter and backtender) were not complex while the press was running, with some important exceptions during set-up, color change and quality control. For example, when the cutter set-up the rewind roll, he did this by winding masking tape around the rolls, then rotating it so that it was in contact with the high-speed plastic film being turned out by press. He watched the counter for a specific yardage count. When the counter read 1200 yards (approx.), he cut the moving plastic sheet with a sharp knife so that the "running" film was attached to the pick-up roll. He reset the counter, moved the completed roll onto a dolly, then installed a new empty pick-up roll in anticipation of the next splice. He then waited approximately 15 minutes for the next roll. This was his *basic* job.

It was physically hard work. Most of the cutter's errors occurred in failing to make a complete cut, i.e., the running plastic was not separated (producing wastage). This task occupied somewhere on the order of 80% of his time and, if there was a very long run of several thousand yards, it was his only duty.

Use of the JTA technique lent itself to the classification of several aspects of the worker's duties within the crew-machine operation, as follows: (a) the *crew functions*, those performed in consort with the other two members at the work station; (b) the *process*, those relating to the recording (or like) duties, given the observation that the machine was providing the primary function of heat, and temperature control and ink flow; and (c) the *operation*, those relating to machine tending, feeding and off-bearing. These are shown in Table D.3, classified (as above) for both cutter and backtender.

Middle Phase of JTA

The scope of the JTA effort in this phase leads to the posing of certain questions and to providing appropriate responses, as follows:

1. *Question:* Why were more experienced men at work at the seemingly easier job of cutter?

Response: By tradition, the cutter (since he waited for the roller to become fully wound or he waited for the machine to be set-up for unprinted goods or for a new production run) was now required to do other things. He watched color registry of the printed "goods" as it came off the press, assisted in the loading of unprinted goods (with the help of the backtender or printer), and helped in the set-up of engraved rollers (heavy, bulky, and awkward to set in place).

Responsibilities of the backtender were complex. He controlled the ink supply, doctor blade, and roller tension. Despite the fact that these tasks took longer to learn (proficiency was generally achieved in about 6 weeks), new employees were frequently started in this position.

As with the cutter, the backtender's basic job had been attenuated and expanded to cover some of the printer's work, such as ink mixing, color registry, and so on.

Another aspect of the organization of production was that new employees often were *not* started at the simple tasks. Instead, they were placed at the more difficult backtender's job. Because the cutter was located at the opposite end of the press away from the printer, the backtender could more readily be helped by the printer. The printer could not readily see the cutter unless he left his printing position. As a consequence, new employees were directly assigned to the backtender's job under the supervision of the printer. The implication that followed from this observation was that there was more flexibility inherent in the production process than was initially apparent.

If the reason for starting the new man at the backtender position was related to training and interim supervision, then the training program to be developed would need to solve this problem, i.e., perhaps both men in the crew could be thought of as assignable to either cutter or backtender positions after training.

2. *Question:* Which aspects of the job, if done poorly, would cost the company money or hamper production, those aspects which would have to be "protected" in a training design?

Appendix D

Response: The aspects of the job which were necessary to the protection of production, either by saving costs or in avoiding damage, were: (a) cutting without waste, without slowing down the machine excessively while training the man, (b) performing *all* quality control operations, (c) performing the set-up and color change quickly, and (d) taking care not to damage the expensive rollers.

3. *Question:* What was the potential for overlapping more of the lower skill with the higher skill tasks of the printer?

Response: There was some overlap of functions between printer and crew during set-up and color change. These overlaps were used to redesign the lower level jobs by shifting these printer duties to the cutter and backtender (under his supervision). Historically, these encroachments on the printer's job were sometimes made to speed up production during changeover. More formally, they were specified, increased in scope, then assigned to the cutter and backtender. This allowed them to learn these parts of the press and their functions in an ordinated way. During the running of the press, while tending, their knowledge of inks, its properties and viscosity, were increased to thereby provide information about the principles and controlling variables of printing plastics.

*

These observations and data lead to the redesign of the cutter and backtender jobs (shown in Tables D.3 - D.6). This new, combined job was called *cutter-backtender*, composed of three sub-components: (a) a *basic* job, essentially cutting; (b) a *tending* job, essentially quality control, feeding materials and controlling parts of the press as needed at each job station; and (c) a *first level print* job, consisting of set-up and color change (as before), plus certain additional duties, some of those normally performed by the printer during changeover.

To achieve this realignment of job tasks, the printer's job was studied in detail. From this, a determination was made of the feasibility of reassigning part of his job tasks to the cutter-backtender. As a first step, the job description for the printer was reviewed (see Table D.7). There was the dual problem of analyzing the job itself as well as its relationship to other jobs in the crew. This was further complicated by the fact that his duties were not accurately described, i.e., they were grouped under several headings, none of which appeared similar to the cutter or backtender's. On further analysis, it became clear that there were different skill levels of greater or lesser responsibility. For example, the printer's job required a considerable knowledge of plastic printing principles and theory, considerable experience in press control, some knowledge of the ink absorbing properties of different materials, as well as color brilliance and contrasts.

As a consequence of a JTA analysis, "core" printer functions were identified. Mainly, these consisted of those duties performed at the front of the press, while the press was running, not during set-up or color change. It was determined that these aspects of the printer's job could be "transferred" over to the combined job of cutter-backtender. This constituted a *first level* print experience, supported by training (see Figure D.1).

Mixed Training Model

The training model supporting the new job of cutter-backtender consisted of classroom instruction (vestibule training at the Training Center), plus on-the-floor OJT supplied by a skills trainer, in that the printer was able to provide only some instruction while performing his job. Briefly outlined, the training plan for cutter-backtender was as follows:

The new hire was shown how to do the *basic* job, right away, at the Training Center. A set of instructions were provided. The *cutting* was simulated. By the time he got to the factory floor, he knew the job sufficiently to produce less wastage, less than would result from "breaking him in" in the traditional manner.

As soon as he learned this aspect of the job, concurrently with his work on the floor, he was moved into the next phase, helping in the *tending* job, e.g., in threading the press. Here, he began to learn the more technical aspects of the job over a period of the next six classroom sessions, supported by an OJT trainer on the factory floor. He was also instructed in the first level printer tasks. A *Cutter-backtender Manual* was used to support the training.

Upon completing cutter-backtender, the new hire could move into the final instructional stage, that of *print trainee*.

213

Figure D.1
REDESIGNED WORK STATIONS

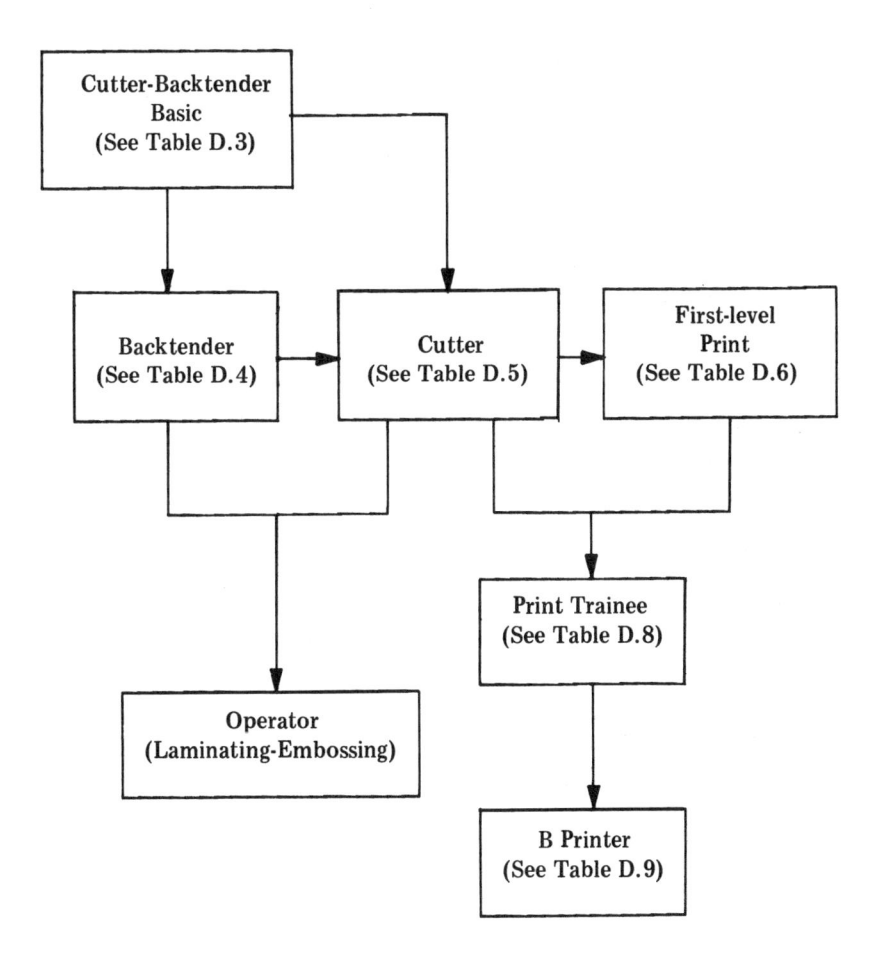

```
┌─────────────────┐
│ Cutter-Backtender│
│      Basic      │
│ (See Table D.3) │
└────┬────────┬───┘
     │        │
     ▼        ▼
┌─────────┐ ┌─────────┐ ┌──────────┐
│Backtender│→│ Cutter  │→│First-level│
│(See Table│ │(See Table│ │   Print  │
│   D.4)  │ │   D.5)  │ │(See Table│
│         │ │         │ │   D.6)   │
└────┬────┘ └────┬────┘ └────┬─────┘
     │           │           │
     │           │           ▼
     │           │      ┌──────────┐
     │           │      │Print Trainee│
     │           │      │(See Table │
     │           │      │   D.8)   │
     │           │      └────┬─────┘
     ▼           ▼           ▼
┌────────────────────┐ ┌──────────┐
│     Operator       │ │ B Printer│
│(Laminating-Embossing)│ │(See Table│
│                    │ │   D.9)   │
└────────────────────┘ └──────────┘
```

Final Phase

The JTA was also used as an analytic instrument in redefining the new printer job and in defining the *print trainee* job. (Tables D.8 and D.9 provide a JTA for the print trainee and printer, respectively.)

As noted, the job of *print trainee* incorporates many of the functions formerly performed by the printer. Those not performed by the trainee were delimited to those the printer does at his job station. (Table D.9 details the *core functions* reserved for the printer.)

Subsequently, during his last phase of training, the print trainee was given progressively greater responsibilities at the printer's station, learning the operation of the press.

At the outset, when *not* assigned as a print trainee (three days per week), he worked as a cutter-backtender. When assigned to print trainee instruction (two days per week), he spent four hours each day in classroom instruction and four hours in formal OJT. Thereafter, on completing the first phase of training, the print trainee was assigned to a crew as a supernumerary (he became the fourth member of a three-man crew). His skills, when ordered, covered some of the printer's work, such as ink mixing, color registry, and so on. From the point of view of maintaining production first and print training second, it provided the print trainee with the beginning fundamentals, those necessary to understanding the operation of the press with the least disruption in production. During the last phase of training, the skills to be learned were staged so that the print trainee was able to perform all the tasks necessary to sustain production, while (at the same time) he was learning to understand the more difficult operations of the press. Then, he was progressively given responsibility for operation of the press (replacing the printer).

Credentializing the New Jobs

The redesigned printer's job did not require new credentials or a title change. Because the printer continued to perform his regular duties, no wage adjustments were involved. The cutter-backtender job did require union-management sanction, especially at the point where the cutter-backtender became a print trainee. There were no recognized trainee positions in the union contract.

Appendix D

Alpha had three printer positions listed in their union contract: (a) assistant printer, (b) B printer, and (c) A printer. In analyzing the printer's function, it was clear that the basic difference between assistant printer and B printer was essentially one of responsibility, not one of job skill (see Table D.10). As a consequence, it was possible to designate the print trainee job as a separate job, but one already recognized by contract because of its relative similarity to the assistant printer title. (The full title and grade of assistant printer was *not* used because of the large number of trainees performing as print trainees. In short, the arrangement was informal but binding.)

Table D.1
JOB DESCRIPTION FOR CUTTER[a]

1. Must read and understand dye order.

2. Must understand and check yardage per combination colors, against orders and clock reset techniques.

3. Must cut neatly and quickly, making wrap on a new core correctly.

4. Must adjust tensions to control roll size as directed on dye order.

5. Must accurately record proper yardage on each roll, together with roll number on label or tape.

6. Must remove finished roll and stack properly without damage.

7. Must keep area under their control clean and neat.

8. Must control film and guiders for mill edge.

9. Must control spreaders for lay-flat and to eliminate creases or foldover.

10. Must assist backtender when required for input of raw materials.

11. Must assist in color changes, pan cleaning and making of new dams.

12. Must assist backtender and/or printer in set-ups and roller changes.

13. Must be able to help put knife into position without damage to roller.

14. Must inspect and signal printer promptly on imperfection in printing such as:
    | Border | Damages |
    | Smears | Registration |
    | Scratches | Side-to-side variations in color |

(a) Table D.1 is the Alpha job description for the cutter. It is reproduced without change.

Table D.2

JOB DESCRIPTION FOR BACKTENDER[a]

1. Must be able to read dye order and select correct raw film, including color, yield width embossing, etc.

2. Must keep accurate record of raw material input on proper forms.

3. Must control position of roll for border control.

4. Must make proper splice and splice on time.

5. Must keep area under his control neat and clean at all times.

6. Must be able to set knives in position without damage to rolls.

7. Must assist in color changes, including cleaning ink pans, and filling new pans with proper ink.

8. Must control ink pumps correctly.

9. Must keep ink fed to nip positions on his side of the machine (except No. 7 printer).

10. Must mount new rolls correctly as to direction of rotation and position on mandrel.

11. Must assist printer to meet target in changing color, set-ups and roller changes.

12. Must be able to make and position dams properly.

13. Must be able to add the proper amount of solvent to ink while running.

(a) Table D.2 is the Alpha job description for the backtender. It is reproduced without change.

Table D.3
JOB TASK ANALYSIS FOR CUTTER-BACKTENDER (BASIC)

FUNCTION	PROCESS	OPERATION
Taking Instructions, Helping	Recording	Tending
Attends to work assignments under orders of printer. Responsible for immediately stopping the press if (a) in an emergency involving possible injury to self or others and (b) any circumstance which would cause wastage.	Completes his portion of the label, noting total yardage (cumulative) and yardage for each roll.	Cutter: 1. Operates the semi-automatic rewind stand and cuts material from running roll; attaches the tail to a new core. 2. Resets individual roll clock-counter to zero. 3. Resets total clock-counter, if order is complete. 4. Adjusts tension for new roll.
Serving		Backtender:
Tends to the needs of the printer. (Printer is in charge of the crew and bears final responsibility for all goods produced. In training, the trainer works with the trainee, informing the printer as to the set up he requires, e.g., slowing down the press.)		1. At the end of the run resets total clock-counter to zero. When order is complete, gives total yardage in writing to printer. 2. Operates hand-wheel to achieve border control.

FUNCTION	PROCESS	OPERATION
		Offbearing

Cutter removes rolls from rewind stand to pallet, stacking them neatly to insure safety. (At his discretion, he may require help in stacking goods on the pallet.)

Feeding

1. Backtender mounts new rolls on stanchion, either using pulley or getting assistance from other members of crew.
2. Backtender affixes tape to new roll, attaching stationary roll to running web on time. |

Table D.4
JOB TASK ANALYSIS FOR BACKTENDER

FUNCTION	PROCESS	OPERATION
Taking Instructions, Helping	Comparing	Handling, Feeding
Attends to work assignments under orders of printer. Works with the dye order, label. Verifies goods as to type, yard, etc. Works independently unless otherwise instructed by printer.	Checks labels on raw films against dye orders for: (a) type, (b) color, (c) yield, (d) width, (e) embossing.	1. Mounts new rolls using pulley or obtains assistance of other crew members. 2. Applies tape to film and splices film to running web on time.
Serving	Copying	Tending
At printer's direction, assists him in performing functions on an as needed basis, e.g., holds air hose, watches printer while he performs dangerous function in order to insure safety, etc. Note: this helping function is independent of the common job and is served both by the cutter and backtender under the direction of the printer only.	Records yardage for each roll fed into machine.	1. Controls ink pumps on his side of the press. 2. Maintains ink level in nips for each color. 3. Under the direction of the printer, adds solvent to ink to achieve proper viscosity.
	Computing	Controlling
Responsible for immediately stopping the press if (a) in an emergency involv-	1. Computes total footage for each color of the run, for total or part as designated on the dye order. 2. Totals yardage of all rolls run for each color and verifies it against the dye order.	1. Operates hand-wheel to achieve border control.

FUNCTION	PROCESS	OPERATION
ing injury to self or others and (b) any circumstance which would cause wastage.		2. Responsible for informing printer if he detects creases, fold-overs, etc. Must immediately inform the printer if he suspects any change in the "look" of the goods as it passes his station.

Table D.5
JOB TASK ANALYSIS FOR CUTTER

FUNCTION	PROCESS	OPERATION
Taking Instructions, Helping	Verifying	Handling
Attends to work assignments on orders of printer. Works with dye order, label, etc. Verifies goods as to type, yard, etc. Works independently unless otherwise instructed by printer.	Checks specifics for finished roll on dye order. Verifies specifics for each finished roll as to: (a) diameter, (b) tension, (c) yardage. Note: he must check each finished roll for each combination of colors.	Sets up rewind stand by mounting core and attaching tape.
Serving	Recording	Offbearing
At printer's direction, assists him in performing functions on an as needed basis, e.g., holds air hose, watches printer while he performs dangerous function in order to insure safety, etc. Note: this helping function is independent of the common job and is served both by the cutter and backtender under the direction of the printer only. Responsible for immediately stopping the press if (a) in an emergency involving injury	1. Records the yards for each roll on the label. 2. Records the total yardage for each combination of colors as specified on the dye order and furnishes the information to the printer.	1. Operates semi-automatic rewind. 2. Cuts goods from running web and attaches tail to new core. 3. Moves finished goods from the rewind stand to pallet, stacking them neatly to insure safety.
		Tending
		1. Operates hand-wheel (a) to maintain proper tension and (b) to control the size of the roll. 2. Adjust spreaders to eliminate creases and fold-overs.

FUNCTION	PROCESS	OPERATION
to self or others and (b) any circumstance which would cause wastage.		3. Adjust guiders to center goods on the roll. 4. Responsible for keeping area in his immediate area neat and clean for maximum safety. Controlling Though quality control is the primary responsibility of the printer, the cutter is in the best position for observing the finished goods. He reports to the printer any creases, foldovers, smears or faults in registration he observes from his station. This might also include detection of such faults as blocking or markoff.

Table D.6
JOB TASK ANALYSIS FOR FIRST LEVEL PRINT, CUTTER-BACKTENDER

FUNCTION	PROCESS	OPERATION
Taking Instructions, Helping	Note:	Note:
Attends to work assignments on orders of printer. Works with the dye order, label, etc. Verifies goods as to type, yard, etc. Works independently unless otherwise instructed by printer.	All processing is determined by the printer. He specifies which inks, coppers, etc., are to be broken out or set up. He will likely utilize the cutter and backtender to assist him in this function. Neither the cutter nor the backtender are to carry out the function independently.	Both the cutter and the backtender perform the functions noted below in assisting the printer. The operations noted in this column refer only to those functions which are accomplished individually by either the cutter or backtender. Though they are expected to be familiar with the operations contained in Table VII, they bear no responsibility for them.
Serving		Handling
Job is accomplished during breakdown and set-up only, under the direct supervision of the printer. The sequence of operation is set by the printer and verbally provided to the cutter and backtender. A typical function to be served by the cutter or backtender would likely involve the following: (a) getting the proper ink from the ink room, (b) exchanging the ink, (c) exchange coppers, and (d) webbing the press.		1. Help bring coppers to the press. 2. Deliver ink to the press. 3. Make and position dams and plugs. 4. Web the press. 5. Make new drains. 6. Position the doctor blade.

FUNCTION	PROCESS	OPERATION
		7. Make and position the flag (sample).
		8. Remove old copper and mount new.
		Feeding
		1. Pour new ink into pans.
		2. Affix new tape to blanket to restrict print area.
		Offbearing
		1. Clean ink pans and pumps.
		2. Remove tape from blanket.
		3. Clean blanket, if necessary.
		Tending
		1. Adjust ink pumps to maintain ink level in pans.
		2. Adjust the spreaders and guiders.

Table D.7

JOB DESCRIPTION FOR PRINTER [a]

1. Must read and understand dye order, yardage requirements and film requirements.

2. Must schedule various films within combinations for proper operation.

3. Must be able to distinguish color combination instructions correctly and make certain that correct product is run and labeled.

4. Must be responsible for set-ups and breakdown; must direct and assist backtender and cutter in setting up and breaking down jobs and color changes.

5. Must know and execute proper rotation, positioning and correct gear engagement on each copper.

6. Must be able to stone doctor blades correctly and pitch blades for printing requirements.

7. Must set and control film tensions properly.

8. Must direct the setting of all spreaders, heat rollers if used, and guiders on machine.

9. Must dilute inks, with correct solvents for efficient operation and consistent product results required.

10. Must maintain color fidelity through the entire run.

11. Must maintain registration throughout run in accordance with dye order requirements.

12. Must furnish active leadership and direction to his crew, instructing them when necessary in the proper exercise of their functions.

(a) Table D.7 is the Alpha job description for printer. It is reproduced without change.

Table D.7 (cont'd)
JOB DESCRIPTION FOR PRINTER

13. Must add inks and solvents on his side of machines.

14. Must be responsible for color match, registration and fidelity to standard sample.

15. Must inspect sample from each roll, compare it to original, initial and stamp the sample.

16. Must be finally responsible for the quality, registration, color, quantity and speed of production of product.

17. Must keep his area neat, and make certain that his crew keep their areas neat and clean.

18. Must assign proper and usable skids.

Table D.8

JOB TASK ANALYSIS FOR PRINT TRAINEE

FUNCTION	PROCESS	OPERATION
Taking Instructions, Helping	Verifying	Handling
Note: Analysis is NOT divided into low, medium and high. Skills are organized in the order in which they would normally be performed, starting with the machine at a full stop. The print trainee is the extra man on the crew and thus has no operational assignment. He may be asked to help by the printer or he may be shown how to perform a function either by the printer or the OJT trainer. This function occurs generally when the machine can be slowed down. Because of the technology involved, complete shutdown is complicated, involving a costly setup procedure. This would not apply during down time. Down time is defined as time taken to maintain the machine or during changeover (frequently referred to as set-up).	Once the printer has completed this function, the trainee goes over the dye order with the OJT trainer. They are only concerned with the dye order as it affects the print department, including the following: 1. Identify color combination to determine the color combination to run first and in what order. 2. Verify total yardage and yardage for each combination. Coordinating With the supervision of the OJT trainer, he analyzes the process the printer goes through to accomplish the following: 1. Deciding sequence of goods to be processed.	Having completed his classroom training, he would be permitted to supervise the cutter-backtender during setup. He might also accomplish the rough registration, the final registration remaining as the printer's responsibility solely. This latter function can only be performed under the direct supervision of the OJT trainer. The trainee would normally perform the following functions under the supervision of the OJT trainer. However, he would not be responsible for these operations until his two-week trial period. These operations are: 1. Responsible for setup, including scraping the blanket, setting gauges, tension, etc.

FUNCTION	PROCESS	OPERATION
The print trainee is not expected to function as a psuedo printer. Generally, he will be asked to perform any one of the functions noted in this table with supervision. From time-to-time, under the supervision of the OJT trainer (NOT the printer), he may perform a series of functions. To accomplish this, the OJT trainer may slow down the machine or perform any other function required of the training situation. Checking The OJT trainer (or printer) would accompany the trainee to the copper room. There they would check with the copper man to check that the correct cylinders were delivered to the press. Thereafter, they would check with the ink man to make sure the proper inks, in accordance with the sample, were delivered to the press. Checks raw stock delivered to the press for proper footage, type, embossing, etc.	2. Deciding on reason as to film inks, etc. if the standard cannot be maintained. 3. Decides on reasons for minor faults, such as breaks, streaks, etc. Analyzing 1. During the run, he observes the printer as the printer directs the crew. He tries to ascertain how the printer evaluates the various criteria which go into meeting the standard noted on the dye order. 2. He checks a swatch from each finished roll with the OJT trainer. At a later stage, they check the swatches against the sample and try to analyze the difference, if any, between the two.	2. Responsible for stoning doctor blade. Controlling Initially, he should perform this operation under the supervision of the OJT trainer. Later, after he has completed his classroom training, he can perform the following functions by himself, but it would have to be rechecked by the printer before starting up the press: 1. Checks all gauges. 2. Inspects blanket. 3. Checks spreaders and guiders. 4. Checks film tension. 5. Checks to see that all gear-wheel covers are secure. 6. Checks ink pumps and ink in nips. 7. Checks pressure rollers. 8. Finally, he ascertains that each man of his crew is at his proper station and able to function.

FUNCTION	PROCESS	OPERATION
Serving	Recording	Manipulation
With the printer's permission, he gives the flag to the ink supervisor. He makes sure that the ink man verifies the correctness of the inks on the flag.	With the printer's permission, he notes the following information on the print production card: 1. Names of crew members. 2. Time of operation. 3. Dye order number. 4. Ascertains and records reasons for stopping the machine during any part of that run.	During the running of the press, the trainee would not be permitted to perform the functions noted below. He could only perform these operations when the press is under the control of the OJT trainer. These include: 1. Checks position of doctor blade for ink control. 2. If necessary, adds solvents to obtain correct ink viscosity and to maintain proper hue. 3. During set-up, the printer makes a rough registration, but before the start of the run must make final registration. Checks registration against the sample.
Supervising	Informing	
Having learned the responsibilities involved in the classroom, he would observe the function of the printer on the floor as he performs the following: 1. Printer provides verbal instructions to members of his crew. 2. Printer assists crew, where necessary, in the performance of their duties. He observes the printer as he reviews the quality of work for all members of the crew. He tries to ascertain how the printer relates to members of the crew. Any questions he may have are directed to the OJT trainer.	During the classroom period, he has learned the function of the centrollograph, a device for signaling the starting and stopping of each operation. In practice, he would observe the printer performing this task.	

Table D.9
JOB TASK ANALYSIS FOR PRINTER

FUNCTION	PROCESS	OPERATION
LOW		
Taking Instructions, Helping	Verifying	Handling
Takes directions from the print supervisor and receives samples from print supervisor. Generally, orders are not delivered verbally but are given on the dye order. As a rule, the only instructions given verbally would concern the order of the color run, a decision that would be made jointly by the print foreman and printer.	Identifies color combination to determine which color combination to run first and in what order. Verifies total yardage, and yardage for each combination.	Supervises cutter and backtender in set-up, except for registration, which is the printer's responsibility solely.
Checking	Recording	Tending
Checks with COPPER MAN to insure the correct cylinders are delivered to the press. Checks with INK MAN to insure the proper inks, in accordance with the sample, are delivered to the press. Checks the flag against the sample. (The sample	Notes appropriate information on print production card, including names of crew, time of operation, dye order number, etc. Records completion of order by using figures furnished by cutter.	1. Any member of the crew can stop the press, but only the printer can start it. The printer must signal the start of the press by blowing the horn. 2. Adds ink on his side of the press.
	Informing	
	At the start of the run, he utilizes centralograph to signal start of operation.	

Note: Table D.9 describes the job as reorganized by NCSI. Supported by PRINTER'S MANUAL.

FUNCTION	PROCESS	OPERATION
comes from the strike off room. The flag results from the actual printing process. By comparing the two, he can intelligently inform the ink man whether the specification is being met.) Checks raw stock delivered to the press for proper footage, type, embossing, etc.

Informing

Meets with crew to inform backtender of the correct scheduling of raw stock and cutter on specifications of finished rolls. On special orders, would indicate whether goods were to be dusted, whether there were any special ink requirements, etc. Checks to see that the cutter picked up the proper labels from the print supervisor.

MEDIUM

Serving | (Centralograph is used to inform production department of all press activities.) | |
| 1. Meets with ink room supervisor to inform him of any change required by | 1. Directs the whole of the run, constantly evaluating various criteria to

Analyzing | 1. Checks all gauges.
2. Inspects blanket.

Controlling |

FUNCTION	PROCESS	OPERATION
the color match. The printer is responsible for maintaining the match only after it has been approved by the print foreman. 2. In the event of trouble, printer meets with foreman, maintenance man, and possibly designer to analyze the fault. He should be familiar enough with the whole process to help in determining the nature of the fault. This is a particularly acute problem because most faults only show up in operation.	maintain and meet standard. 2. Obtain swatch from each finished roll and checks it against the sample. The standard is most difficult to determine during the run, since the machine may be operating in excess of 90 yards-per-minute. As to whether the specifications are being met can only be determined as a consequence of experience, e.g., moving his eyes in a vertical direction he can simulate a strobe effect and the pattern appears momentarily to stand still, permitting him to check the registration and to determine that the color fidelity is correct.	3. Checks spreaders and guiders. 4. Checks film tension. 5. Checks to see that all gear-wheel covers are secure. 6. Checks ink pumps and ink in the nips. 7. Checks pressure rollers. 8. Finally, he ascertains that each man of his crew is at his proper station and able to function. Manipulation 1. Checks position of doctor blade for ink control. 2. If necessary, adds solvents to obtain correct ink viscosity and to maintain proper hue. 3. During set-up, the printer makes a rough registration, but before the start of the run must make final registration. Checks registration against the sample.

FUNCTION	PROCESS	OPERATION
HIGH		
Supervising	Coordinating	Handling
1. Provides verbal instructions to members of his crew. 2. Assists them, where necessary, in the performance of their duties. 3. With new men in particular, helps in their instruction and is supportive to forestall apprehensiveness. 4. Tries to forestall problems in order to maintain standard. 5. Responsible for reviewing quality of work of all members of his crew, leading to recommendations for higher level assignments with additional pay.	1. Decides sequence of goods to be processed. 2. Suggests revisions as to film, inks, etc. if standard cannot be maintained. 3. If break or other fault occurs during the run, determines the reasons for the fault, correcting it if minor. If not, makes suggestions to the print foreman as to how the fault might be corrected.	1. Responsible for set-up, including scraping the blanket, setting gauges, tension, etc. 2. Responsible for stoning doctor blade. Tending 1. Responsible for operation of the press to maintain standard. 2. Periodically checks the work of other crew members. 3. Obtains materials for next run, including deliveries of coppers, inks, and goods to the press. Controlling Responsible for maintaining quality control. Periodically inspects the goods for foldovers, markoff, smears, or faults in registration.

Table D.10
JOB DESCRIPTION FOR ASSISTANT PRINTER[a]

1. Must read and understand dye order, yardage requirements and film requirements.

2. Must schedule various films within combinations for proper operation.

3. Must ascertain color combination instructions correctly and make certain that correct product is run and labelled for each individual dye order.

4. Must direct and assist backtender and cutter in setting up and breaking down jobs and color changes.

5. Must add inks and solvents in nip on both sides of machines.

6. Must keep his area, including pit, neat and make certain that his crew keep their areas neat and clean.

7. Must know and execute proper rotation, positioning and correct gear engagement on copper.

8. Must set and control film tensions properly.

9. Must maintain color fidelity through the entire run.

10. Must be able to do rough pattern registration.

11. Must make and position dams.

12. Must assist in set-ups, changes and color changes.

13. Must relieve printer as required.

(a) Table D.10 is the Alpha job description for the assistant printer. It is reproduced without change.